DELE ALLI

MATT AND TOM OLDFIELD

ULTIMATE FOOTBALL HEROES

DELE ALLI

FROM THE PLAYGROUND
TO THE PITCH

DINO

First published by Dino Books in 2020,
an imprint of Bonnier Books UK,
The Plaza,
535 Kings Road,
London SW10 0SZ
Owned by Bonnier Books,
Sveavägen 56, Stockholm, Sweden

🐦 @dinobooks
🐦 @footieheroesbks
heroesfootball.com
www.bonnierbooks.co.uk

Design and typesetting by www.envydesign.co.uk

Paperback ISBN: 9781789462425
E-book ISBN: 9781789462432

British Library Cataloguing-in-Publication Data:
A catalogue record for this book is available from the British Library.

Printed and bound in Great Britain by Clays Ltd, Elcograf S.p.A.

1 3 5 7 9 10 8 6 4 2

For all readers, young and old(er)

Matt Oldfield delivers sports writing workshops in schools, and is the author of *Unbelievable Football* and *Johnny Ball: Accidental Football Genius*. Tom Oldfield is a freelance sports writer and the author of biographies on Cristiano Ronaldo, Arsène Wenger and Rafael Nadal.

Cover illustration by Dan Leydon
To learn more about Dan visit danleydon.com
To purchase his artwork visit etsy.com/shop/footynews

TABLE OF CONTENTS

ACKNOWLEDGEMENTS

First of all, I'd like to thank Bonnier Books UK –
and particularly my editor Laura Pollard – for
supporting me throughout and for running the ever-
expanding UFH ship so smoothly. Writing stories
for the next generation of football fans is both an
honour and a pleasure.

I wouldn't be doing this if it wasn't for my brother
Tom. I owe him so much and I'm very grateful for
his belief in me as an author. I feel like Robin setting
out on a solo career after a great partnership with
Batman. I hope I do him (Tom, not Batman) justice
with these new books.

Next up, I want to thank my friends for keeping

me sane during long hours in front of the laptop. Pang, Will, Mills, Doug, John, Charlie – the laughs and the cups of coffee are always appreciated.

I've already thanked my brother but I'm also very grateful to the rest of my family, especially Melissa, Noah and of course Mum and Dad. To my parents, I owe my biggest passions: football and books. They're a real inspiration for everything I do.

Finally, I couldn't have done this without Iona's encouragement and understanding during long, work-filled weekends. Much love to you.

CHAPTER 1

HOMETOWN HERO

26 September 2018, Stadium MK

It felt good to be back. Three years after his big transfer to Tottenham, Dele was returning to Stadium MK, the place where his amazing football adventure had started. He was returning as a Premier League star and Spurs captain. His manager, Mauricio Pochettino, had given him the armband for his special homecoming.

Dele wouldn't be playing against his old club MK Dons, however. No – Tottenham were taking on Watford in the Carabao Cup. But while their new stadium was being built, they had to play their home games elsewhere. Usually, that was Wembley, which wasn't available for this match. So, for one night only, Dele was back home, kicking off in Milton Keynes.

As he led the Tottenham players out onto the pitch, Dele's mind was filled with many happy memories of Stadium MK:

His first goal against Cambridge City,

His first hat-trick against Crewe Alexandra,

Thrashing the mighty Manchester United 4–0,

And finally, winning promotion to the Championship.

Despite Dele's many achievements since then, that League One runners-up trophy was still the only one that he had ever lifted as a professional player. Hopefully, however, he was going to make the Carabao Cup his second piece of silverware.

Fortunately, the first big chance of the game fell to… Dele! After spreading a lovely ball out wide to Serge Aurier, he sprinted towards the six-yard box, as he loved to do.

'Yes!' Dele called out.

But instead, Serge passed to Lucas Moura, who swivelled and fired the ball across goal. It flew all the way through to the back post, but for once, Dele wasn't quite quick enough to react.

'Nooooo!' he sighed. What a chance to be a hometown hero again!

Never mind, there would be more chances to come. With fifteen minutes to go, Tottenham were losing 1–0, and on their way out of the Carabao Cup. But Dele couldn't let that happen, especially not on his special night as team captain.

So when Érik Lamela passed him the ball, Dele drove powerfully into the box, with only one thing on his mind – scoring a goal. But as he took a second touch, he was tripped by a Watford defender. *Penalty!*

There was no Harry Kane in the Tottenham team that day, so Dele stepped up to take it himself. Pressure? What pressure?! He had no doubt that he would score. With a deep breath and a short run-up, Dele swung his right leg at the ball. The keeper dived the right way, but the spot-kick landed safely in the bottom corner. *1–1!*

*Goooooooooooooooooooaaaaaaaaaaaaaaaalllllllllllll
lllllllllllll!!!!!!!!!!!!!!!!!!!!!*

'Yesssss!' Dele roared, looking up at the sky and
then up at the celebrating Spurs supporters.

He wasn't a true hometown hero yet, though, not
unless Tottenham won. Érik gave them a 2–1 lead,
but then in the last minute, Watford equalised. There
would be no extra-time; the match went straight
to penalties.

Dele would take one, of course, but he didn't go
first. Instead, he went fourth, once the expectations
were even higher. By then, Son Heung-min, Érik and
Fernando Llorente had all already scored for Spurs.
And their keeper, Paulo Gazzaniga, had already
made two super saves to deny Étienne Capoue and
Domingos Quina.

So this was it: Dele's chance to win it for
Tottenham and show that he was still a hometown
hero. After placing the ball down on the spot, Dele
took two big steps back, keeping his eyes focused on
the target. He wasn't afraid of anything, especially
not match-winning moments like this.

Again, he aimed low for the bottom left corner, and again the keeper couldn't stop it. *GOAL!* Tottenham had won 4–2 on penalties – they were through to the next round!

'Nice one, mate!' Érik shouted as they high-fived happily.

Dele played it cool as he turned away to celebrate, but inside he was buzzing with pride and joy. On his emotional return to Stadium MK, he had scored two spot-kicks to win the tie for Spurs.

After shaking hands with all the Watford players, Dele walked around the pitch, clapping for the fans. Most had come from Tottenham, but some were locals who had bought tickets to welcome back their boy wonder.

'Thank you!' he called out to the crowd.

No matter how many Premier League, Champions League and World Cup matches he played in, Dele would always be that kid from Milton Keynes with the mischievous grin.

CHAPTER 2

CREATING CHAOS AT
HEELANDS COURTS

'Look who's back, lads!' one of the men called out during a drinks break at Heelands Courts. Together, the footballers turned and watched as a little boy walked determinedly through the council estate and up to the court. 'Wow, he's brave, I'll give him that.'

'Good to see you again, kid!' one of the players said with a smile as the boy entered the cage. 'Ready for Round Two?'

Dele nodded eagerly.

'Great, we thought we might have scared you off after last time!' joked another.

Dele shook his head very seriously. No way, it would take a lot more than some big, strong men to scare him. Especially when it came to playing his new favourite game – football.

Karl, one of the captains, clapped his hands. 'Okay, same teams as before, but we'll take …sorry, what's your name again?'

'Dele,' the boy replied. 'Dele Alli.'

'That's right – Dele's on our team. Right, shall we get started again?'

Suddenly, Karl seemed to remember that he was a responsible adult, even on the football court. 'Wait, your family does know where you are, right?' he asked.

Again, Dele nodded his head eagerly. It was only a half-lie – his mum, Denise, did know that he was outside playing somewhere around the council estate, just not *exactly* where. She wouldn't mind, though; in fact, she'd be pleased. Because if Dele was on the football court, that meant that he was getting some exercise *and* staying out of trouble.

His dad had moved away when Dele was only a baby, leaving him to live with his mum, half-brother and two half-sisters in Bradwell, Milton Keynes.

It was a busy household and a difficult place to be sometimes. So even at the age of seven, Dele was already used to doing his own thing and looking after himself. That's why he was there at Heelands Courts, about to play another game of football against big, strong men.

'Yes, pass it!' Dele called out confidently after running into space.

When he had first started playing, his teammates had just ignored him, but now they trusted him with the ball.

Dele controlled it with the side of his right trainer, all the while looking and listening to the sights and sounds around him.

'Back to me, mate!'

'Over here, Dele!'

'Come on, close the kid down!'

When he had first started playing, his opponents had gone easy on him, but now they treated him like any other player. That was a sign of respect, especially for a seven-year-old boy. It showed that they believed he had the toughness *and* the talent to compete.

However, that respect made it much harder for him. Dele knew that if he took too long on the ball, the other team would use their superior size and strength to swoop in and tackle him. And his own teammates would not be happy about that at all.

Dele had to either play a simple pass or do something special. Those were his two options, but which one would he choose? He knew that his teammates wanted him to keep things simple and safe, but the more he played, the more confident he felt, and the more fun he wanted to have.

Entertainment – that's what football was all about, right? He loved watching and then teaching himself all the stylish skills he saw out on the court – the tricks, the flicks, the million different ways to beat a defender. They might not work every time, but how would he know unless he gave them a go?

So after faking to pass it, Dele spun and slid the ball straight through the defender's legs. *Nutmeg!*

He carried on running to reach the ball on the other side, but by then, the game had already stopped. With that cheeky bit of skill, Dele had created total chaos at Heelands Courts.

'Woah, Danny, are you alright? That kid just SCHOOLED you there!'

'Mate, check your pockets – I think he just stole your self-respect!'

'Nutmegged by a kid – that's a new low for you, lad!'

'Dele, I hope you're ready for Danny's revenge!'

A cheeky smile spread across Dele's fearless little face. Of course, he was ready for anything.

CHAPTER 3

CITY COLTS

As Dele got a bit older, he decided to leave Heelands Courts behind and travel a bit further in search of football fun. One Sunday morning, he went down to a nearby park to watch his friends play for a local youth team called City Colts.

When he saw the players lining up together as a team, wearing their matching kits, Dele thought to himself, 'Cool, I want to do that too!'

Dele was only eight years old at the time, so he didn't yet understand how club football worked. He hoped that it would be the same as the cage games at Heelands Courts, where he could just turn up and ask:

'Excuse me, can I play please?'

Unfortunately, it wasn't that easy. Mike Walsh, the manager of the City Colts Under-9s, looked at the eager young boy in his tracksuit and frowned.

'Sorry, son, this is a league game,' he explained. 'You have to be registered with the team in order to play.'

Dele nodded glumly but he didn't give up. 'I'm really good at football, I swear!' he pleaded.

The Colts manager liked the boy's self-confidence. 'I'm sure you are, kid! But I'm afraid I still can't let you play – not today anyway. Listen, why don't you come and train with us next week and we'll take a look at your skills?'

Dele nodded again, but this time, a lot less glumly. 'Thanks, see you then!'

By the time the next Colts training session started, Walsh had all but forgotten about that offer. Dele, however, had remembered. He had been thinking about it all week and now he was back and ready to show off his skills.

'Hello again!' the manager welcomed him warmly,

before turning to the rest of the squad. 'We have a new player joining us for training this week... sorry kid, I don't even know your name!'

'Dele,' he replied. 'Dele Alli.'

It was a name that Walsh would never forget. Within minutes, the Colts manager had seen enough to know that Dele was the real deal. Where had he learned to play like that? The boy's touch was brilliant and so was his movement, both with and without the ball. But best of all, was his unique style. For such a young kid, Dele played the game with such confidence and creativity. He loved taking risks and trying new things.

When they played a match, Dele nutmegged the Colts' previous best player, flicked the ball over the next defender's head and then volleyed it in. *GOAL!*

'Wow!' was all Walsh could say on the sidelines. Was there anything that this kid couldn't do? He was watching a future professional footballer; he knew it already.

'You were right,' Walsh said with a smile at the end of that first training session. 'You are *REALLY* good at football. I'm very glad you came back today!'

A fearless little grin spread across Dele's little face. 'Me too, Coach!' He couldn't wait to start playing for his new team.

Playing for City Colts wasn't just about being good at football, however. It was also about a sense of belonging and working together as part of a team. Walsh was a manager who cared about his youngsters. He wanted to help them develop as players but also as people. He now knew what Dele was like on the pitch, but what about off the pitch?

Walsh learnt more about his new superstar when he started picking him up and dropping him off after training. Dele told him about the cage matches at Heelands Courts against bigger, older boys:

'So, that's where those skills come from – and that toughness!'

Walsh saw signs of the boy's sometimes difficult home life in Bradwell. It all made the Colts manager realise that he had to handle his promising young player with care.

Most of the time, it was all happiness and trophies. With Dele as their new Number 10, the Colts became almost unbeatable. He had the magical ability to win matches on his own, dribbling his way through whole teams as if it was the easiest thing in the world.

GOAL!

ASSIST!

GOAL!

At times, however, it was all *too* easy for him. And if a match wasn't much of a challenge, then Dele would try to create new challenges for himself. In one game, he even jumped onto the ball and tried to balance there for as long as possible!

'Any more showboating like that and I'll have to send you off,' the referee warned him.

'Sorry!'

With Walsh's help, Dele was becoming a better team player, but he still didn't always like being told what to do. Sometimes, there were strops and sulks at training, which led to time-outs on the sidelines.

'Why can't I just play the way I like to play?'

'No, I don't want to do that. You can't make me!'

But those grumpy moods never lasted long. In no time, Dele would be back out on the pitch again, doing what he did best – playing stylish football with with a big grin on his face.

CHAPTER 4

STEVIE G AND BIKES FOR GOALPOSTS

'The ball falls to Gerrard, who strikes it first time from distance, *BANG!...*'

With those words, Dele fired off a shot that flew past the keeper and just missed the bike that they were using as a goalpost, in the local car park that they were pretending was Wembley.

'...*GOOOOOAAAAALLLLL!*'

Dele celebrated by patting the back of his jacket, right where his name would be on a proper, Premier League football shirt. That's what Steven Gerrard had done after scoring a spectacular late equaliser for Liverpool against West Ham in the 2006 FA Cup

Final. Dele had watched the YouTube clip so many times that he knew it off by heart.

'He's done it…' he called out just like the commentator in the video, '…STEVEN GERRARD!'

'Yeah, well how many Premier League titles has he won then, mate?' jeered the grumpy Manchester United fan in goal as he jogged over to get the ball back.

'Whatever, Stevie's won the Champions League!'

The Liverpool and England midfielder had quickly become Dele's biggest football hero. They played in slightly different positions – Dele was more of an attacking Number 10, whereas Stevie was a box-to-box Number 8. They also had slightly different playing styles – Dele was more about silky skills, whereas Stevie was more about perfect passing. But ultimately, Dele felt like they had lots in common. For example:

1) They both enjoyed every part of the game – passing, shooting and dribbling, but also heading and tackling too. For City Colts, Dele was always chasing back to reclaim the ball with crunching challenges.

He wanted to be involved in everything, at both ends of the pitch.

2) They both loved assists almost as much as goals. Despite his awesome skills, Dele wasn't a selfish attacker. He played with his head up, looking for ways to connect with the strikers. In club football, Dele had learnt that he couldn't just show off his new tricks all the time like he did at Heelands Courts; that didn't win you games, tournaments or league titles.

And best of all:

3) They were both brave, big game players. Another one of Dele's favourite YouTube videos was Liverpool's legendary second-half comeback against AC Milan in the 2005 Champions League Final. And who had started it off, with a brilliant header and then a 'Make Some Noise!' signal to the supporters? Stevie G – what a hero! FA Cup Finals, Champions League Finals, World Cups – no matter how important the match was, he just played the same way he always did, with drive and determination.

'I'm the same!' Dele thought to himself.

Stevie didn't fear any opponent, and neither did Dele. He believed in himself and his ability to beat anyone. With the ball at his feet, he felt unstoppable. Because thanks to all those hours spent in the cage at Heelands Courts, he knew hundreds of different ways to dribble past defenders and score great goals. All he had to was pick which one to go for.

When City Colts needed a match-winning moment of magic, they turned to Dele, and he usually delivered. He had that strong character, that 'I'm not afraid of anything' attitude, on top of his tremendous football talent. What a winning combination! Walsh was right; one day, Dele could play in the Premier League, and maybe even for England, just like his hero, Stevie G. Why not?

The only thing that could stop Dele from achieving that dream was himself. Unfortunately, when he wasn't playing for the Colts or having a kickaround in the car park with bikes for goalposts, he had started hanging around with the wrong crowd.

In Bradwell, it was often difficult for a young boy like Dele to ignore the bad influences around him.

He knew kids in local gangs, who were already involved in crime. For now, though, football was keeping Dele focused on the right path. If he wasn't careful, however, he could end up making bad mistakes and wasting his tremendous talent. Luckily, he had people around him who wouldn't let that happen. Instead, they helped him to make the most of himself, and follow in Stevie G's footsteps.

CHAPTER 5

MOVING TO
MK DONS

In Milton Keynes, 2004 turned out to be a big year for football. While Dele was starting his career at City Colts, just a few miles down the road, MK Dons were starting life as a League One club.

The team formerly known as 'Wimbledon' already played their home games in the town at Stadium MK, but now that they had just been relegated from the Championship, the owners decided that it was time for bigger changes. So, for the new season, the club had a new name as well as a new division to play in.

Exciting times! But while Dele was soon winning tournaments with the Colts, the MK Dons didn't get off to such a good start. In fact, in 2006, the club dropped down into League Two. What a disappointment, both for the Dons and for the town of Milton Keynes!

That same year, however, MK made a very wise decision for the future of their football club. They hired a new youth coach: Mark Walsh, the City Colts manager. And which young superstar did he take with him to his new team? Yes, that's right – Dele!

'It's only a trial at first,' Walsh explained to his ten-year-old wonderkid, 'but I'm sure you'll find a way to impress the other coaches.'

Wow, this was it; Dele's first chance to play at a professional football academy. He couldn't wait for his new challenge to begin. After two weeks of the trial, everything was going according to plan. Dele was playing well and there hadn't been any real sulks or strops. So far. But as the Under-11s prepared for a friendly against Chelsea at Stamford Bridge, Walsh had some bad news for Dele – he wouldn't be able to play in the game.

'What? Why not?!'

All Dele wanted to do was play football – what was wrong with that? It felt so unfair that he had to miss the team's biggest match of the season, just because he was new and not a permanent player yet. Rubbish! It was like that first Sunday morning at City Colts all over again. Before he could control himself, Dele exploded with hurt and anger. 'Fine, I'm done here, and I'm not coming back!'

It took Walsh a lot of time and effort but eventually, he did persuade Dele to come back and play for the MK Dons again. And once he started training four times a week with the club, he calmed down, worked hard and just got better and better and better. It was a joy to watch a kid playing with such confidence and creativity.

'Brilliant through-ball, Dele – you created that chance out of nothing!'

'Well done, lad – that's top work there!'

It certainly helped that Walsh had worked with him before and so knew how best to handle him. Sometimes, Dele needed a bit of detailed, one-to-one coaching, and sometimes he needed his own space to develop his game naturally. Sometimes, he needed an arm around his shoulder, and sometimes he needed an angry time-out.

But most importantly, Dele always needed to be challenged on the football field. If things became too easy, he just got bored. So, every week, Walsh tried to raise the bar a bit higher for him: more goals, more assists, and even more ideas.

'What else do you think you could have done in that position?'

'Erm... play the pass out wide and then make a late run into the box?'

'Good, try that next time.'

Like his hero, Stevie G, Dele had that drive and determination to keep learning and improving. Now that he was a rising star at the MK Dons academy, he was fully focused on football and making the most of his talent. Dele could see a successful career ahead of him, and nothing was going to distract him from achieving his goals.

CHAPTER 6

A NICE NEW HOME WITH THE HICKFORDS

Dele was really loving his new life at the MK Dons academy. What was there not to love about it? He was having loads of fun, playing loads of football, and hanging out with his new friends.

'This is the life, lads!' Dele joked at training. 'Football all day every day!'

Yes, the Under-14s were like a band of brothers, both on and off the pitch. They all got on really well and that showed in their excellent match-day performances. Although there were a lot of promising young players in the squad, they never saw the academy as a talent contest. No, they weren't competing against each other. Instead, there was a real team spirit because they were all trying to make it to the top together, including:

A fast forward called George Williams,

A big centre-back called Brendan Galloway,

A dogged defender called Harry Hickford,

And a midfield magician called Dele Alli.

They were all good friends, but Dele and Harry were *BEST* friends. They clicked straight away and soon they were inseparable. Not only did they play for the same team, but they also went to the same school, The Radcliffe. They spent every day together, talking endlessly about their favourite thing – football, of course!

'Here they are – attached at the hip, as always. Come on, let's go, Tweedledum and Tweedledee!'

Harry's parents, Alan and Sally, got to know their son's best friend very well. They knew that things were difficult for Dele at home, so they kindly took him to the MK Dons matches and then often invited him home for dinner afterwards. Before long, Dele started staying over after dinner, and then he started staying there three days a week, then four, then five... He was part of the Hickford family now and he was hardly going home to Bradwell at all.

'We've been thinking,' Harry's parents said to Dele one day when he was thirteen years old. 'How would you feel about coming to live here permanently? We'll need to check with your mum first, of course, but we'd love to have you and we've got the room if that's what you want.'

'Wow, really?'

Dele was delighted – it was definitely what he wanted. He had been hoping that they would ask him for ages. He loved living with the Hickfords in the nice neighbourhood of Cosgrove, but what about his mum back in Bradwell?

For Dele's mum, Denise, it wasn't easy to let Dele go, but she knew that it was the best thing for him. If he stayed, she would always worry about her son getting into trouble like some of the other kids on their estate. Alan and Sally were good people, who would look after Dele and offer him a safe environment. That was the most important thing for him and for his future football career. The

Hickfords' house was only six miles away, but that was still far enough to leave the bad influences in Bradwell behind.

'Well, I guess we really are brothers now!' Harry said with a smile as he helped Dele move in the last of his belongings.

Dele smiled. 'Yeah, and I'm two months older than you, so don't forget that!'

Now that they lived together, they could start plotting their path all the way to the MK Dons first team.

'In a couple of years, we could be playing for the Under-18s, and then if we do well, we'll get called up to the Reserves, and then League One, here we come!'

At the end of the 2008–09 season, the Dons had won promotion from League Two at last. They had achieved that under the guidance of ex-Chelsea star Roberto Di Matteo, but now the former Manchester United midfielder Paul Ince was their manager again, with Karl Robinson as his assistant.

The most exciting thing for Dele and Harry,

though, was that the club was calling up more and more of their most talented youth players. Sam Baldock had made the move from the academy to the first team in 2007 and now he was their star striker. After that, many more followed: Adam Chicksen, Tom Flanagan, David King, Daniel Powell, and Sam's brother, George Baldock.

'And we'll be next!' MK Dons' brand-new 'brothers' declared confidently.

As he settled into his nice new home with the Hickfords, Dele felt more determined than ever to achieve his dream of becoming a professional footballer.

CHAPTER 7

SIZE AND SKILL

Even in that talented MK Dons youth team, Dele still stood out head and shoulders above the rest. It was clear to anyone watching that he was a truly special player with truly special skills. On the ball, he could do things that the others didn't even dream of.

A scoop pass to a striker – *Olé!*

A flick over a midfielder's head – *Olé!*

A nutmeg through a defender's legs – *Olé!*

A back-heel shot past a goalkeeper – *Olé!*

'That kid's not afraid to try anything, is he?' laughed the Dons' youth team director, Mike Dove, full of admiration.

To some, it might have looked like arrogance, but

it wasn't really. It was just Dele's unique combination of confidence and creativity. He played football for fun and without fear. He backed himself to find a way out of any tricky situation, any tight space on the pitch. His head was full of new ideas and if a trick failed the first time, he didn't just give up on it. No, he would try it again and again until it worked perfectly. Dele had first developed his skills playing street football back at Heelands Courts, and now he was taking them to the next level at MK Dons.

'If we coach him well, that kid could become a real superstar!' thought the Under-15s manager, Dan Micciche.

However, Dele's arrival coincided with his reaching a difficult age. Suddenly, all the kids around him were growing taller and stronger – everyone except him. And if you were thirteen years old, football wasn't just about your skill anymore; it was also about your size.

That meant Dele was at a big disadvantage. Now, when he tried to dribble past defenders like normal, they could just push him off the ball.

'Hey!' Dele protested, but the referee shook his head. 'No foul – play on!'

With every minute, Dele was getting more and more frustrated up front. He wanted to be on the ball all the time, trying out his usual tricks, but that was impossible when his opponents kept barging him out of the way!

'Ref!'

What was he supposed to do when he was so much smaller? The good old days of street skills were officially over; Dele needed to find a new way to win matches for MK Dons, and fast. It was size that seemed to matter most, so why wasn't he growing big and strong like everyone else?

'Don't worry, your time will come,' Micciche tried to reassure him.

'Okay, but when?'

Dele didn't want to wait around. His best friends Harry and George had both already had their growth spurts and now they'd been called up to Under-16s. They were on their way to the first team without him! Football just wasn't as much fun anymore.

Micciche could see that Dele wasn't happy. He had lost his flair and his fearlessness too. Where was that desire to improve?

'Hey, size isn't everything,' Micciche reminded Dele one day when he was looking particularly miserable at training. Hopefully, some extra motivation would help cheer him up. 'Look at Maradona – he's only five-foot five and and he's one of the greatest footballers of all time! He didn't let his size stop him, did he? No, he just worked on his skills until he could escape from even the biggest, baddest defenders!'

Dele nodded his head, his determination returning. His manager was right; he was too good to just give up now and let big defenders boss him around. He was an intelligent player, with lots and lots of ideas. He could overcome this new challenge.

Until he grew taller and stronger, Dele would just have to work harder to outsmart his opponents and be more creative than ever. For now, he had to forget about what his friends were doing and focus on becoming the best footballer he could be.

'Always think one step ahead, before you even get the ball,' Micciche coached him. 'Pass and move, pass and move. Play it as early as possible – that way, they can't tackle you!'

'Look for that space between their midfield and defence. Keep searching until you find it!'

'And use your pace as well – that's another powerful weapon! Mix it up, with bursts of speed at just the right moment.'

Dele listened carefully and learned quickly. But it was when Micciche moved him into a deeper midfield role, that everything really fell into place. Suddenly, he had that extra bit of time and space to pick his pass or create some magic. Perfect!

By the time Dele turned fifteen, he had become a better footballer and a bigger, stronger one too. All of a sudden, he had shot up to six-foot tall and he wasn't finished growing yet. Hurray! At last, he had the skill *and* the size – surely there was nothing stopping him now.

With a huge 'Thanks!' to Micciche, Dele moved up to join Harry and George in the Under-16s, then the Under-17s, and then the Under-18s...

...Because Dele was back and better than ever! Once again, he was the top young talent that the whole club was talking about. Before long, word had spread all the way to Karl Robinson. After one season as Ince's assistant, he had been named as the new MK Dons manager in May 2010.

Robinson was on the lookout for promising young players to promote to the first team. And when he went to watch Dele play for the first time, he could hardly contain his excitement.

'Wow, this kid is going be a superstar!' Robinson boldly predicted.

CHAPTER 8

TRAINING WITH THE FIRST TEAM

It was fortunate that Dele had got his fearlessness
back because ahead of the 2011–12 season,
Robinson decided to call up three young players to
train with the MK Dons first team:

George,

Brendan,

And Dele!

This was an extremely big deal, especially
for fifteen-year-olds. Were they really ready for
this? They would be boys amongst men! As
they arrived at the training ground, George and
Brendan both looked a bit nervous, but not Dele.
He had a mischievous grin on his face as usual.

He was determined to make an unforgettable first impression...

When the three youngsters entered the dressing room, the senior players stopped talking and turned to look.

'Great, some more shy, quiet kids to play against!' thought Darren Potter, the experienced Dons midfielder.

Darren had seen it so many times before: talented young players who turned up at training with the first team but were too worried about making mistakes to actually do anything impressive. Then after a few awkward sessions, they disappeared back to the academy.

Well, that's what usually happened at MK Dons, but Darren was about to meet a different kind of talent. Dele wasn't going to change his game just because he was training with the big boys now. This was his chance to prove himself on the pitch, like at Heelands Courts all over again. Confidence and creativity had got him this far, and now these qualities would get him into the first team too. So, in the first few minutes, when Darren came over to tackle him, Dele coolly slid it straight through his legs. *Nutmeg!*

Woooooaaaaah! Had the new kid really just embarrassed an experienced pro like that? Where was the respect? There was stunned silence all over the field. Dele carried on playing, as if it was nothing special, but he knew that his plan had worked. The senior players had certainly noticed him now.

'That boy is BRAVE!' was their first thought, but as the session went on, they added an extra bit:

'And BRILLIANT!'

After that first cheeky nutmeg, Dele didn't switch to keeping things safe and simple. No, he carried on showing off his full range of skills. A flick pass here, a back-heel there, a dribble between two defenders to score. *GOAL!*

So this was the new wonderkid that everyone was talking about – he was making professional footballers look like fools! Well, it was time to see whether the boy could cope with a bit of physicality.

A push here, a shirt-pull there, a crunching challenge from behind. *FOUL!*

Dele didn't complain and he didn't back down. He just picked himself up off the grass each time and carried on fighting for the ball. It would take more than a few strong tackles to scare him.

As Robinson watched from the sidelines, a big smile spread across his face. Talent? Tick! Toughness? Tick! Yes, Dele definitely had something special about him. And with a few more years of development, he would be ready to become a superstar.

During the 2011–12 season, Dele didn't quite get to make his debut for the MK Dons first team, but he trained with the squad regularly, and he was a sub for all of their FA Cup matches. That turned out to be an exciting, but also frustrating experience. The good news was that he got his very own shirt number – 36 – and the chance to feel like part of the first team. The bad news was that Dele had to do two of his least favourite things in football – watching and waiting.

When the Dons went 5–0 up in the First

Round against Nantwich Town, Robinson turned to his youngsters on the bench. He still had two substitutions left to make...

'Pick me! Pick me!' Dele muttered under his breath, moving his legs around restlessly.

But instead, Robinson decided to bring on George and then Brendan. Noooo! When George scored a sixth goal in the ninetieth minute, Dele was pleased for his friend, but he couldn't hide his own disappointment.

'That could have been me!' he thought to himself.

Sadly, there was no space for youngsters in their Second Round win at Barnet, or in their Third Round defeat to QPR.

Oh well, Dele's MK Dons debut would definitely come soon – during the next season for sure. Until then, he just had to keep working hard in training, and show Robinson that he was ready to shine brightly for the first team.

One day, the players were practising a new corner routine. As the cross came in, it was Dele's job to make a run to the front post and jump up to get the flick-on.

'Right, let's give it a go!' Robinson called out, clapping his hands together.

But as Dele made his move towards the front post, he could see that the cross was coming in at the wrong height for a header. Never mind, he would just have to use his incredible creativity. After all, he had the confidence to try anything. In a flash, he turned his body and volleyed the ball into the net with the heel of his boot. *GOAL!*

Extraordinary! As everyone stared at him in disbelief, Dele decided to celebrate by performing a second skills show with his chewing gum. He juggled it:

From one knee, to the other knee,

Then from the right foot, to the left foot,

And then for a finale, he flicked it up and caught it in his mouth again. *Ta-da!*

'Mate, that's disgusting!' George joked as they got ready to try the corner routine again.

'I think what you mean is – that's different class!' Dele replied with a cheeky grin on his face.

CHAPTER 9

TWO DARING DEBUTS

A year on from that disappointing day at Nantwich Town, Dele was back on the bench for MK Dons in the FA Cup First Round. This time, they were playing Cambridge City and Dele had the number 21 on his back, plus Harry and Brendan there to keep him company.

'Let's hope we thrash them,' they agreed as the game kicked off, 'because then we might get some game-time at the end!'

But as the second half went on, the score stayed at 0–0, and Robinson started to wonder what changes he should make...

'Pick me! Pick me!' Dele muttered, moving his legs around restlessly again.

His hopes were a lot higher for this match. He was sixteen now and he was one of only two attackers on the MK Dons bench: the other was the former Leeds United and Manchester United forward, Alan Smith, who was now more of a central midfielder. So, if the manager wanted a match-winning moment of magic, then Dele was his man.

'Alli, get ready,' he heard one of the coaches call out, 'you're coming on!'

At last, Dele's MK Dons debut had arrived! With a quick 'Good luck!' high-five from his friends, he made his way down to the touchline.

Substitution for MK Dons. Replacing Number 23 Jay O'Shea, Number 21 Dele Alli...

'Who? Who?' the Cambridge City fans jeered.

Dele had about thirty minutes to prove himself and make sure that they remembered his name. As he ran onto the field, he didn't feel nervous at all. Why would he? He was playing first-team football for the first time! This wasn't something to worry about; this was fun and exciting.

'Yes, over here!' Dele cried out, racing into space. He wanted to be on the ball as much as possible.

And when it came to him, what next? Well, Dele wasn't interested in playing safe, simple passes. What was the point of that? So instead, his very first touch was a back-heel.

'What was that?!' On the touchline, Robinson looked like he was ready to tear his hair out. A back-heel? What did the boy think he was doing – having a casual kickaround with his mates? The Dons weren't winning 6–0; they were drawing 0–0 against a non-league team! If Dele didn't start taking it seriously, he would be back on the bench...

The next time the ball came to him, Dele fooled the defender by letting it roll across his body, and onto his stronger right foot.

'Yes, yes, yes!' Robinson thought, his excitement building.

Dele could hear two teammates calling for the pass but instead, he decided to go for goal on his debut, from thirty yards out. Why not? He believed in himself.

'No, no, no!' Robinson groaned as Dele pulled his leg back and unleashed the shot. Luckily, it took a deflection and went out for a corner, because otherwise he would have been in big trouble with his manager.

Once he had calmed down a little, Robinson couldn't help admiring his young player's confidence. Nothing fazed Dele, not even making his first-team debut at the age of sixteen. When it came to football, the kid was totally fearless.

By the time the final whistle blew, Dele had shown more flashes of his bravery and brilliance, but it wasn't enough to change the score line of 0–0. The Dons would have to do better in the replay back at Stadium MK.

And Dele would have the chance to do better on his full debut. Yes, Robinson had seen enough in those thirty minutes to think that his young star was ready to play from the start. So when the teamsheet was revealed, there was his name and number – '21 ALLI'

– alongside Stephen Gleeson in central midfield.

'Good luck!' his manager told him before kick-off. 'Don't let me down.'

And Dele didn't. He played with the determination of a sixteen-year-old, combined with the composure of an experienced pro. With his help, the Dons dominated the game and put in a much-improved performance. They were 3–0 up by half-time and late in the second half, he even scored a stunning strike to complete a fantastic full debut.

When Dean Lewington passed the ball to him, Dele was at least thirty-five yards away from goal. It would have to be an absolute beauty to beat the keeper from there, but why not? It was worth a hit. For him, nothing felt impossible. This time, the Dons were winning 4–1, so he knew that his manager wouldn't mind. Dele shifted it onto his right foot and *BANG!* The ball flew through the air like an arrow, past the Cambridge City defenders and all the way into the top corner of the net. *5–1!*

Goooooooooooooooooooooaaaaaaaaaaaaaaaalllllllllll llllllllllllllllll!!!!!!!!!!!!!!!!!!!!!

'Wow!' marvelled the 4,000 supporters at Stadium MK that night.

Dele started jogging back to the halfway line as if it was no big deal, but his teammates weren't going to let him get away without a proper celebration.

'What a worldie!'

'Congrats, kid!'

'You won't score a better one than that, mate!'

'Stevie G, eat your heart out!'

They cheered, wrapping a delighted Dele in a big group hug.

What a proud moment – the first of many great goals, hopefully! It felt like the start of something really special.

And Robinson, the MK Dons manager, agreed. On the bench, he smiled and turned to his coaches. 'What did I tell you? That kid is going to be a superstar!'

CHAPTER 10

REGULAR STARTER AT SEVENTEEN

After his cracker against Cambridge City, Dele went on to make five more first-team appearances across all competitions. He wanted to play for MK Dons every week, of course, but he didn't mind waiting as long as he was moving in the right direction.

'Dele's a very special player,' Robinson told the media at the end of the 2012–13 season. 'He's going to go right to the top of English football and we've just got to make sure we nurture him in the right way.'

So, did that mean Dele would get to play fifteen matches next year? Or maybe even twenty? That might have been the plan at first, but not after Dele's phenomenal preseason. While other players were slowly getting back in shape after their summer holidays, he was looking fitter, stronger and fiercer than ever. Whatever challenge the coaches set, he always fought his way to the top. Dele had found a new gear, and now he was unstoppable.

'Man, do you ever stop moving?' Darren panted as he tried his best to mark his young teammate in training. 'You're an absolute machine!'

Dele gave his most mischievous grin. 'Come on, keep up – or do you want me to nutmeg you again? Just be glad that we play for the same club, mate!'

Everyone at MK Dons was very impressed with Dele's development – especially their winger, Luke Chadwick who, back in 1999, had been part of Manchester United's amazing Treble-winning squad under Sir Alex Ferguson. Luke had played with Premier League legends like David Beckham, Ryan Giggs and Paul Scholes, and he could see that Dele shared many of the same qualities. The speed, the skill, the desire – but above all, the self-belief. He played with confidence, like he could achieve anything.

'You're not afraid of anyone, are you?' Luke laughed as Dele battled for the ball against Tom, the Don's biggest defender. 'If you can play like that in League One this season, then the top clubs will soon come calling!'

That sounded super exciting, but Dele was taking things one step at a time. For now, he was focused on starring for his local, boyhood team. For a promising young player, MK Dons was the perfect place to be. He could play without pressure, and he was sure to get a lot more game-time there. The club had just given him the Number 14 shirt, a clear sign that he was creeping closer and closer to that First XI.

Ahead of the opening game of the new season, Robinson announced that Dele would be starting alongside Darren and Stephen in midfield. No-one at MK was surprised by that news, not after preseason. Yes, he was still only seventeen, but Dele was a superstar in the making.

'Up you go, kid!' With Darren in a deeper role behind him, Dele had the freedom to get forward as much as possible. He wasn't yet producing magic every week, but the more he played, the more consistent and creative he became. By the time Stevenage arrived at Stadium MK, Dele was looking really dangerous.

With twenty-two minutes played, Patrick Bamford, their striker who was on loan from Chelsea, was already on a hat-trick, and he was on the attack again. This time, though, he looked up and spotted Dele on the left, making a bursting run into the box.

'Yes!' he called out, pointing towards the penalty spot.

At first, Patrick's pass looked a little too heavy, but determined Dele wasn't giving up. He slid across the grass and stretched out his long left leg to bring the ball under control. What next? He didn't have enough time to get back up before a defender closed him down, so instead he took the shot from on the floor. What quick, creative thinking! It wasn't his most powerful strike, but it was enough to catch the keeper out.

Goooooooooooooooooooaaaaaaaaaaaaaaaaalllllllllllll llllllllllll!!!!!!!!!!!!!!!!!!

His first league goal! Dele raced over towards the corner flag to celebrate. Soon, he was at the bottom of a big pile of players.

'Next time, can you play a better pass?' Dele joked with Patrick as they jogged back to the centre-circle. They were forming a strong friendship, as well as an excellent strike partnership.

'Nah, next time, I'm taking the shot myself!'

In the second half, Dele won a penalty, which Shaun Williams scored to make it 4–1. When MK's young stars were at their best, they could beat anyone in League One.

Sadly, Patrick's loan spell ended in January, but by then, Dele was ready to make the step up from regular starter to regular scorer.

In the opening minutes against Shrewsbury Town, he chased after Stephen's through-ball and headed it bravely past the keeper. *1–0!*

Away at Notts County, Jordan Spence's long pass bounced down in the boggy penalty area. While the players around him panicked and miskicked, Dele calmly slotted the ball into the bottom corner. *1–0!*

'Nice one, we needed a bit of class there!' their striker Izale McLeod said with a smile.

And early in the second half, Dele was on the scoresheet again. Daniel Powell pounced on a poor back pass, dribbled forward and then played it across to his teenage teammate. *2–0!*

'Cheers, mate!' Dele shouted as he threw his arms out wide. There were only 3,000 fans at Meadow Lane that night, but one day soon, he would be celebrating in front of much bigger crowds.

It was Dele 2, Notts County 0. Could he add a third goal and complete his first professional hat-trick? Yes, he could, with another assist from Daniel. In the last minute, his chipped pass landed at Dele's feet, on the left edge of the penalty area.

In the middle, Izale was calling for the cross, but Dele had a different idea. The final whistle was just seconds away, but he dribbled into the box as if he had all the time in the world. Then with a quick look-up, Dele curled a shot past the keeper, and past the diving defender on the line too.

*Goooooooooooooooooooaaaaaaaaaaaaaaaaalllllllllll
lllllllllllllll!!!!!!!!!!!!!!!!!!!!!!*

What a moment! His eighteenth birthday was still
one month away, and Dele was already a professional
hat-trick hero. Unbelievable! With his right arm
up high in the air, he raced away to celebrate. He
couldn't wait to take that match ball home with him.

'The game's been won by a wonder boy,' Robinson
declared afterwards, with no doubt in his mind.
'He's one of the most gifted seventeen-year-olds this
country has ever seen.'

Wow – if England's top teams hadn't already heard
the name 'Dele Alli', well they definitely had now.

CHAPTER 11

MANCHESTER UNITED MASTERCLASS

26 August 2014, Stadium MK

Although promotion to the Championship was MK Dons' top priority for the 2014–15 season, a fun cup run was always a nice bonus. After beating bitter rivals AFC Wimbledon in the EFL Cup First Round, they now faced one of the most famous clubs in the world – Manchester United.

Oh boy, this was a big one! But Dele didn't feel nervous; he was going to treat it just like any other game. In the Dons dressing room, he went through his same old routine:

Right sock, then right boot (size 10), then right

shin pad (the same ones he had worn since he
was eleven years old), left sock, then left boot (size
10-and-a-half), then left shin pad...

Right, he was ready! Ready to raise his game. Behind that calm, fearless face, Dele couldn't wait for the most important match of his career so far. He was already a star in League One; now, this was the next step, his toughest challenge yet. With the TV cameras watching, he was determined to prove himself against top Premier League players.

The new Manchester United manager Louis van Gaal had decided to rest his biggest stars like Wayne Rooney, Juan Mata and Robin van Persie, but there was still plenty of talent in their team. Their two starting strikers, Danny Welbeck and Chicharito, had scored over fifty Premier League goals between them. Goalkeeper David de Gea and midfielders Anderson and Shinji Kagawa had all cost about £20 million each, and then there was Nick Powell, the 'next big thing' United had signed from League Two club Crewe Alexandra for £6 million.

'Well, we'll see about that,' Dele thought to himself as the two teams walked out for kick-off.

From his very first touch, Dele took confident control of the game. He passed and moved, passed and moved, all over the pitch. At the age of eighteen, he was putting on a midfield masterclass and United couldn't handle him.

When they tried to get physical, he showed that he could make tough tackles too. *CRUNCH!* Poor Powell wasn't going to forget the day when he first played against Dele Alli. He wasn't afraid of anything or anyone. Jonny Evans tried to outmuscle him in the box, but Dele went shoulder to shoulder with him and came away with the ball.

'Hurray!' the MK Dons fans cheered when their boy wonder won the battle.

Dele was everywhere, enjoying his time in the spotlight. One minute, he was back heading away a United corner, and the next, he was at the other end, taking a long-range shot.

'Unlucky!' Robinson encouraged from the sidelines. 'Keep going!'

Whenever a teammate looked up to play a pass, there was Dele, calling for the ball, with lots of space and time. MK Dons were doing brilliantly; now they just needed to score a goal...

Halfway through the first half, United made a mess of things at the back. As Evans took his time on the ball, Ben Reeves raced in to close him down. Not only did he block the pass, but Ben also then got to the rebound first, cutting it back for Will Grigg to score. *1–0 to MK Dons!*

'Get in!' Dele cheered as he rushed over to celebrate with Will and Ben. The Cup upset was on!

It stayed 1–0 until midway through the second half. By that time, some of the MK players were starting to slow down, and their fans were starting to fear the worst.

Not Dele, though. He wasn't tired and he certainly wasn't scared. With cool confidence, he kept calling for the ball and swapping neat one-twos with his teammates. As much as Dele loved to get forward and attack, Robinson had given him a different, deeper role to play that day. He had to show discipline alongside Darren in the middle and help protect the defence.

'Come on, nothing's getting past us, okay?'

When Evans flicked the ball on into the MK six-yard box, it was Dele who reacted first to hook it away, high into the air. And by the time it eventually dropped, he had rushed out to the edge of the area, to steal the ball from Michael Keane before he could shoot.

'Hurray!' the fans cheered. Was there anything that Dele couldn't do? What an amazing all-round player he was!

As the minutes ticked by, MK Dons just had to hold on, and hope for another Manchester United mistake…

At last, it arrived. On a quick counter-attack, Ben delivered a perfect cross to Will, who somehow chested the ball past De Gea. *2–0!*

Yes! A second goal was just what MK needed to calm things down, and there were even more to come.

Benik Afobe came off the bench to finish off a brilliant team move. *3–0!*

'Yes, mate!' Dele cheered as they did a little dance together by the corner flag.

And then Benik dribbled his way through the United defence to score again. *4–0!*

Wow, what a night, and what a thrashing! And yet even in the very last minute, Dele was still battling for the ball and chasing back to help the defence. His team had a clean sheet to keep. Only when the final whistle blew, did he stop and breathe and punch the air. Job done!

'We just beat Manchester United!' Dele cried out in disbelief.

Benik smiled and shook his head. 'No mate, we just *BATTERED* Manchester United!'

Dele asked to swap shirts with Welbeck, but the striker had already offered it to someone else. Oh well, nothing was going to ruin his night to remember. Although every single Dons player deserved so much credit for an excellent team display, there were some clear, stand-out performances:

Will and Benik, who had both scored two goals each,

Ben, who had grabbed three amazing assists,
And most eye-catching of all,

Dele, the confident young pass master who had outplayed the whole Manchester United midfield.

Back in 2003, United had been battered by another amazing eighteen-year-old – a skilful winger called Cristiano Ronaldo. After that game, Sir Alex Ferguson had signed him to the club straight away. Dele wasn't as lucky, but lots of other big clubs were interested in him.

CHAPTER 12

POCHETTINO IMPRESSED

Among the many football scouts and coaches watching Dele's Manchester United masterclass, was Mauricio Pochettino, the new Tottenham manager. He was so impressed by what he had seen that he went straight to the MK boardroom after the match.

'That kid is incredible,' Pochettino said with a smile. 'I want him in my team!'

It was a former Spurs manager, David Pleat, who had first spotted Dele's potential and recommended him to Pochettino.

'He's really athletic, he runs up and down all game long, and he's strong in the air too,' Pleat wrote in his scouting report. 'Plus, he seems very mature for such a young player.'

Interesting! Tottenham already had a top goal scorer in Harry Kane and a creative playmaker in Christian Eriksen, but what they were still missing was that box-to-box energy in midfield. They needed someone with skill and speed, but also power and determination. And the more that Pochettino watched Dele play, the more he knew that he would be perfect for the role. He knew this because, outside the box, Dele played like a clever midfielder, but once he stepped inside, he became a clinical striker.

After finishing his first full season with seven goals, Dele had set himself much higher targets this time around.

GOAL! A tap-in against Peterborough.

GOAL! A cheeky chip over the keeper at Barnsley.

GOAL! GOAL! GOAL! Another hat-trick for Dele, this time against Crewe – one leaping header and two quality right-foot finishes, plus a beautiful assist for Benik.

'Too easy!' Dele joked with his teammates, but it

was true. He was getting too good for League One now and everyone knew it. Although he had just signed a new contract until 2017, there was no way that Dele would stay that long at MK. It was time for him to test himself at a higher level.

And it was time for Tottenham to make their move before it was too late. Because lots of other clubs were keeping a close eye on Dele, including Aston Villa, Newcastle United, Bayern Munich and his favourite team as a kid, Liverpool. They had even invited Dele to come to Anfield, hoping that a chat with his hero, Steven Gerrard, might persuade him to sign.

'Wow, I'm going to meet Stevie G!' Dele thought excitedly, like he was ten years old again. However, when he arrived at Liverpool, Gerrard was nowhere to be seen.

'Sorry, he's sleeping ahead of our big game tomorrow,' the club explained.

Oh well, never mind – it was still a good chance for Dele to go behind the scenes at one of the biggest clubs in the world. As he looked around, everything looked so massive, modern and amazing, especially compared to MK. It really would be a dream come true to play at a stadium like Anfield, in front of 50,000 fans.

However, as Liverpool paused to think, Tottenham jumped ahead to take the lead. Pochettino had found the box-to-box midfielder that he was looking for, and he didn't want to wait until the summer, and maybe miss out on signing Dele.

'Let's do the deal now,' he told the Spurs chairman, Daniel Levy, during the January transfer window.

When he heard the news, Dele was delighted. A proper offer from a Premier League club? That was his dream come true. 'I'm in!' he told his agent immediately.

'Woah, woah, woah – slow down!' he replied. 'Take your time and think about what you really want.'

Okay, well, Dele wanted to play for a top team, and Tottenham was certainly one of those. They had just finished sixth in the Premier League, which meant they would be playing in Europe too.

Dele also wanted to play for a top manager, who

believed in him and wanted to help him become a better footballer.

For that, he knew Pochettino would be perfect. The Argentinian had a great record of improving players at Southampton – Luke Shaw, Adam Lallana, Morgan Schneiderlin, Calum Chambers, Jay Rodriguez, Dejan Lovren… the list went on and on.

But Dele didn't want to go and sit on the bench at a big club. That would feel like a step backwards after over eighty first-team games for MK Dons by the age of eighteen. He wanted to play as many games as possible. He decided to talk about it with Pochettino.

'Don't worry, I don't see you as a player for the future,' Pochettino promised Dele when they met to discuss the deal. 'If you sign for us, you'll go straight into the Spurs first-team squad. And if you keep working hard and impressing the coaches, then you will get plenty of chances to play.'

Dele nodded his head happily; that was exactly what he wanted to hear. He understood that the Premier League was going to be a big step-up, but he was determined to do his absolute best to shine straight away. Like MK Dons, Tottenham was a club that gave their young players plenty of chances – Ryan Mason, Andros Townsend, and of course, Harry Kane.

Okay, deal almost done! Dele only had one more request: 'Can I please go back to MK on loan for the rest of this season?'

He couldn't leave the Dons just yet, not when promotion was a real possibility. At the halfway stage, they were top of the League One table, and Dele had noticed a huge difference in his hometown. Suddenly, there were lots of people walking around, wearing their MK shirts with pride. It was amazing! If Dele could just help his local club to reach the Championship, then that would be the perfect way to say thanks and goodbye, after eight amazing years.

'No problem,' Pochettino told him. 'You go finish what you started, and we'll see you back here next season.'

Agreed! On Deadline Day, 2 February 2015, Dele signed for Spurs for a fee of £5 million.

'It's a massive club and I'm really happy to be here,' he said to the journalists after posing for lots of photos wearing his new club's white shirt. 'I can't wait to play at White Hart Lane.'

It was a deal that suited everyone: Tottenham, Dele, and, of course MK Dons.

'We are immensely proud of Dele,' Karl Robinson told the media, 'and we are delighted to keep him with us for the rest of the season. Hopefully, we can share some more amazing moments, before he moves on.'

CHAPTER 13

LEAVING LEAGUE ONE ON A HIGH

So, could Dele help lead MK Dons back up to the Championship where they belonged? That was the aim, but it wouldn't be easy. With sixteen games to go in the League One season, they had dropped down to third in the table, behind Bristol City and Swindon Town. And with every game that MK failed to win, Preston North End and Sheffield United were creeping up behind them.

'We can't let this slip now!' Robinson told his players. They had to find their best form again, before their promotion dream faded away.

Colchester United sat second from bottom in

League One, but they were still making life difficult for MK Dons on a tense Tuesday night.

'Come on Dele, we need a moment of magic!' the fans urged as half-time approached.

'I'm trying!' he muttered to himself, growing more and more frustrated. It wasn't the kind of game where he could really show off his silky skills. The ball was in the air most of the time, hoofed from one end to the other. But suddenly after three high headers in a row, Antony Kay booted the ball over the top of the Colchester defence...

Dele was onto it in a flash, before the centre-backs could even react. The ball bounced up perfectly in front of him, asking to be blasted into the roof of the net. But what if he got it wrong? In the end, Dele didn't smash his shot past the keeper; no, he calmly passed it into the bottom corner instead. *1–0!*

Goooooooooooooooooooooaaaaaaaaaaaaaaaalllllllllllllllllllllllllllllll!!!!!!!!!!!!!!!!!!!!!

'Yes, Dele!' Carl Baker screamed, jumping on his back.

'What a hero!' cheered Dean, their captain.

That goal turned out to be the matchwinner, but it wasn't all good news for MK Dons. Midway through the second half, Dele felt a sudden pain in his ankle. 'Arghhhh!' He winced as he fell to the floor. Was it a bad injury? It was hard to tell at first. He tried his best to run it off, but the pain was getting worse. Eventually, he had no choice but to hobble off the field and down the tunnel to see the physio.

Robinson crossed his fingers and hoped that it was only a minor knock. Sadly, however, it was a lot more serious than that. MK Dons would be without their main man for over a month, right when they needed him most.

'Six whole weeks?' Dele groaned in disbelief. It was his first proper injury, and that long without football sounded like a lifetime. But thanks to his own hard work and the help of the Tottenham doctors, Dele returned in time for the final eight games.

'I'm back!' he cheered as he entered the dressing room.

There was now a big gap at the top of the League One table between Bristol City and everyone else.

Preston were leading the pack, but there was still plenty of time left to catch them. If the Dons finished second, they would be promoted as well, but if they finished third or fourth, they would be thrown into the tricky play-offs instead.

'We've got to grab that second spot,' Dele said with real determination. 'Let's do this!'

Eighteen from the last twenty-four points – that might be enough to get MK back into the Championship. But they weren't taking any chances, and with Dele back, they went eight games unbeaten, picking up twenty-two points along the way!

Swindon Town 0 MK Dons 3,

MK Dons 2 Scunthorpe United 0,

Port Vale 0 MK Dons 0,

Fleetwood Town 0 MK Dons 3...

In the latter game, Dele set up the first with a cross to Lewis Baker, and then scored the third himself, with a right-foot rocket from the edge of the area.

Goooooooooooooooooooooaaaaaaaaaaaaaaaaaallllllllllll llllllllllll!!!!!!!!!!!!!!!!!!

Meanwhile their rivals Preston could only draw with Gillingham, which meant the gap was now just three points.

'Come on!' Dele roared with pride and passion. They were too good not to go up.

MK Dons 6 Leyton Orient 1

With a drop of the shoulder, Dele fooled the first defender, before curling a beautiful shot in off the post.

Goooooooooooooooooooaaaaaaaaaaaaaaaaalllllllllllll llllllllllllll!!!!!!!!!!!!!!!!!!

Dele's sixteenth goal of the season – Dele made everything look so easy!

MK Dons 3 Doncaster Rovers 0

For once, Dele didn't score himself, but he did set up two goals for Carl instead.

'Cheers, mate!' the striker said, giving him a happy high five.

And there was more good news to follow. Preston had drawn at Port Vale – MK were now only one point behind!

Rochdale 2 MK Dons 3

This was their toughest test, but Dele set up the

winner with a through-ball to Daniel. Yes! The Dons were so close now. It all came down to the final day of the season. They had to win at home against Yeovil Town, and hoped that Preston wouldn't win, away at Colchester.

'We're going up!' Dele declared confidently before kick-off. 'I just know it!'

At half-time, it was so far so good for MK. They were already 4–0 up, whereas Preston were still drawing 0–0. If the scores stayed the same, the Dons would jump up into that precious second spot. However, if Preston scored…

'Come on, Colchester!' Dean shouted across the dressing room.

Dean made it 5–1 to MK in the seventy-fourth minute, but the biggest cheer of the day came eight minutes later. Colchester had taken the lead against Preston! The news soon spread around the stadium.

'Get in!' the MK subs shouted, jumping up and down on the sidelines. That sent a clear message to their teammates on the field.

Would Preston produce an incredible comeback at

Colchester? No, the Dons had done it – they were going up! When the final whistle blew at Stadium MK, there were scenes of total chaos. The supporters stormed the pitch, rushing over to celebrate with their heroes.

'We're the Dons, we're the Dons, we're the Dons…'

'We love you, Dele – please don't leave!'

'WE ARE GOING UP, SAY WE ARE GOING UP!'

'Championship, here we come!'

Dele was so happy for the fans, for the coaches and for his teammates too – they all deserved to share this moment of glory together. It was a dream come true to help lead his local team to promotion.

What a season, and what a way to say goodbye! Dele had delivered big time: sixteen goals, nine assists and thirty-nine awesome performances at the age of just eighteen. Unbelievable! Now, it was time for the new Football League Young Player of the Year to tackle his next challenge – the Premier League.

CHAPTER 14

PREMIER LEAGUE? NO PROBLEM!

Although Dele felt as self-confident as ever, he tried to be realistic about his targets for his first season at Spurs. As much as he wanted to walk straight into Pochettino's starting line-up, he knew that he would have to take things one step at a time. As he looked around the Tottenham training ground, he was surrounded by top-class internationals now:

Harry Kane and Kyle Walker both played for England,

Hugo Lloris was the keeper and captain of France,

Christian Eriksen was Denmark's danger man,

New signing Son Heung-min was the star of South Korea,

Érik Lamela played alongside Lionel Messi for Argentina,

And then there were the boys from Belgium: Jan Vertonghen and Toby Alderweireld in defence, plus Mousa Dembélé and Nacer Chadli in midfield.

That was a lot of talent in one team! And as Dele soon found out, they lived up to their reputation. At first, every session was a school day, with so much for him to watch and learn:

Harry's finishing,

Christian's creative passing,

Mousa's powerful dribbling,

Érik's tricks,

Son's speed...

Dele was the new kid, and he was hanging out with the big boys now. Was he really ready to fight for a starting spot? Yes, he believed in himself, but he would have to be patient and make the most of the opportunities that came along. Ten starts – that was Dele's aim ahead of his first Spurs season. It didn't take long for him to exceed those expectations...

During the summer of 2015, Dele and his
Tottenham teammates travelled to the USA to take
on the MLS All Stars. After that, they journeyed
to Germany for the Audi Cup, one of the most
prestigious preseason tournaments. Their three
opponents that year?

Real Madrid,

AC Milan,

And Bayern Munich.

'Welcome to the big time!' Eric Dier laughed.
Tottenham were playing against a Real Madrid
team featuring such names as Sergio Ramos, James
Rodríguez, and former Spurs duo Luka Modrić and
Gareth Bale.

'Bring it on!' Dele replied with a big grin. It was
no big deal. If he could do it against Manchester
United, then he could do it against anyone. And
although he was still young, he had already played
nearly one hundred first-team games, so he knew
what he was doing.

Dele made a calm and confident start against
the mighty Real Madrid. He kept calling for the

ball and then playing quick, accurate passes to his left and right.

'That's it, mate,' Mousa, his midfield partner, encouraged him. 'You're a natural!'

In the twenty-third minute, Dele got the ball near the halfway line. In his first months at Tottenham, he had already learnt one very important thing – you got a lot less time on the ball at the top level. His first touch had to be perfect, and he had to think one step ahead, otherwise an opponent would rush in and take the ball away...

This time, the opponent was Modrić. Out of the corner of his eye, Dele could see the little Croatian sprinting towards him to make the tackle. No problem! Dele fooled him with his favourite trick. He waited until the last second and then slid the ball straight through Modrić's legs.

Nutmeg!

Wow, that was a very brave move to attempt against one of the best midfielders in the world! But Dele was determined to show that he was fearless on the football pitch. Modrić had the last laugh, however, as Real Madrid won the match 2–0.

That was only preseason, though. Soon, it was time for the main event to start – the Premier League. And who did Spurs face on the opening day of the 2015–16 season? Dele's old friends, Manchester United.

'Oh good, I've played against them before,' he told Eric. 'And we battered them!'

Although Dele started on the bench at Old Trafford, he did eventually come on for the last fifteen minutes.

Substitution for Tottenham. Replacing Number 15 Eric Dier, Number 20 Dele Alli…

This was it – Dele's Premier League debut! He was determined to succeed, determined to make a difference straight away. However, as hard as he fought for his new club, he couldn't change the score line:

Manchester United 1 Tottenham 0

It wasn't the dream Premier League debut that Dele had been hoping for, but two weeks later, Pochettino gave him another chance, away at

Leicester City. And this time, he had a whole thirty minutes to create some magic.

'Let's do this!' Dele told himself with a focused look on his face.

For the next half an hour, he ran and ran, from box to box, just like Pochettino wanted him to. One minute, Dele was helping out in defence, and the next, he was racing forward to help Harry up front.

'Yes!' he called out as he sprinted into space on the right.

Harry passed left to Nacer instead, but Dele kept running, into the Leicester penalty area.

'Yes!' he called out again, now unmarked at the back post.

Nacer's cross flew just over Harry's head, but there was Dele to flick it bravely past the keeper with a diving header. He nearly crashed into the post along the way, but he didn't care about that. He had scored, and that was all that mattered in the moment. *1–0!*

Goooooooooooooooooooooaaaaaaaaaaaaaaaalllllllllllll llllllllllllll!!!!!!!!!!!!!!!!!!!!

Even Kasper Schmeichel sitting on him couldn't stop the smile from spreading across Dele's face. What a feeling, and what a time to get off the mark! As he jumped back up, Harry tried to hug him, but Dele dashed away towards the corner to celebrate with all the Tottenham fans. Premier League? No problem! This was where he belonged. Dele had only played thirty minutes of football in England's top division and he had already scored his first goal.

'Get in!' he screamed, punching the air with passion.

Would he be Tottenham's matchwinner? Unfortunately not, because less than two minutes later, Leicester equalised. The match finished 1–1, but from that day onwards, Dele became a starter for Spurs.

CHAPTER 15

ENGLAND'S EXCITING NEW STAR

'Dele for England!'

Now that he was proving himself in the Premier League, people started talking about that next big step – to senior international football.

Although there had been a bit of interest from Nigeria, the country where his dad was from, Dele had always dreamed of wearing the Three Lions for England. England was where he was born and where he was living, and he was a huge fan of the national team, especially when it came to World Cups and Euros.

Plus, Dele had been rising up through the England ranks for years – the Under-17s in 2012, then the

Under-18s in 2014, quickly followed by the Under-19s, where he starred on his debut against Germany. That day, Dele had been the only League One player in a squad full of Premier League talent:

Chelsea's Ruben Loftus-Cheek,

Manchester City's Angus Gunn,

Leicester City's Ben Chilwell,

Tottenham's Harry Winks...

But when did Dele ever let that stop him? Never! It only made him more determined to do well. In the thirty-fifth minute, he robbed the ball off Mahmoud Dahoud in midfield and poked a perfect pass through to England's striker, Bradley Fewster. *1–0!*

Dele wouldn't stay in the Under-19s for long, though. A year later, Gareth Southgate had called him up to the England Under-21s. And now, just one month after that and making his Premier League debut, he was on the move again...

...up into the senior squad!

It seemed so sudden, but actually the England manager, Roy Hodgson, had been scouting Dele for years. His assistant, Ray Lewington, often went to watch MK Dons matches because his son, Dean, was the team's captain. And that's where he had first come across a sixteen-year-old wonderkid who had everything – strength, power, skill, intelligence *and* desire.

'Dele Alli,' Lewington told Hodgson straight away. 'Remember that name because the boy's going to be big!'

Hodgson kept a close eye on Dele's development at MK Dons and then his early days at Tottenham. 'Yes,' the England manager decided, 'he's ready!'

So for the final Euro 2016 qualifiers against Estonia and Lithuania, there were two new call-ups to the England squad:

Liverpool's Danny Ings…

…And Tottenham's Dele Alli!

Wow, what a proud moment – it was hard to believe that this was really happening to him. Just one year earlier, Dele had been battling for League One promotion, and now, he could call legends like Wayne Rooney, James Milner and Gary Cahill his 'teammates'. It was unreal.

'Congratulations!' messaged Harry Kane, who would be there with him for his special night at Wembley.

For most of the match, Dele sat there on the bench, watching and waiting. As the game entered the last ten minutes, his chances of coming on didn't look good. England were only 1–0 up and Ross Barkley was running the show in midfield. Did they really need Dele?

'Oh well, maybe I'll make my debut against Lithuania instead,' he began to think.

But all of a sudden, Harry flicked a long ball onto Jamie Vardy, who crossed it to Raheem Sterling. *2–0!*

Phew! On the sidelines, Hodgson punched the air. Now he could calm down and think about that last substitute… After a quick discussion, Lewington turned to the bench.

'Dele, get ready. You're coming on!'

His tracksuit was off in an instant, and Dele was standing on the touchline, raring to go, wearing the same Number 20 shirt that he wore for Tottenham.

Sadly, those last five minutes flew by in a flash. As

Dele chested the ball down near the centre-circle, the final whistle blew. But he didn't stop playing straight away; no, he tried a cheeky chip from the halfway line! The Estonia keeper made the save, but it just showed Dele's confidence. He wasn't afraid to try anything, even at international level.

Three days later, Dele played the last thirty minutes against Lithuania, as England made it ten wins out of ten. And what did he do when he first got the ball?

Nutmeg!

It was fun being out there on the pitch, playing for his country, but by then, the game was already over. And with Ross having another great game, how was he going to win a starting spot in midfield? Euro 2016 was now only nine months away, and Dele was determined to get there. But how? He would just have to make the most of England's friendlies before the big tournament.

Dele was a second-half sub again in the 2–0 defeat to Spain, but four days later at Wembley, he finally got the chance to start, against France. Playing in a three-man midfield with Ross and his Tottenham teammate, Eric, Dele would have to show off his full range of skills – in defence and in attack. He even had the Number 7 shirt, once worn by the great David Beckham.

'This is it,' Dele told himself before kick-off. 'My time to shine!'

When he saw Harry battling for the ball against three French players, Dele rushed to the rescue. With a big, brave sliding tackle, he won it back and flicked it forward to Nathaniel Clyne, who passed it wide to Wayne.

By that time, Dele was back up on his feet and calling for the ball again. 'Yes, Wazza – I'm in space!'

When the pass arrived, Dele dribbled forward, preparing for the shot. Yes, he had Ross to his left and Harry up ahead, but this was *his* moment. He believed in himself, and so from just outside the box, Dele took aim and fired.

BANG! He watched with growing excitement as the ball flew past the France defence, and then arrowed towards the top right corner. Would his

Tottenham teammate, Hugo Lloris, be able to stop it? No!

Gooooooooooooooooooooaaaaaaaaaaaaaaaaalllllllllllll lllllllllllllll!!!!!!!!!!!!!!!!!!!!

What a fantastic strike on his full England debut! With his arms out wide, Dele ran towards the fans, finally sliding the last bit of his run on his knees.

'Yesssss!' he yelled out with that with a huge smile on his face.

Dele wasn't done yet, though. Early in the second half, he won another midfield battle, stealing the ball off Paul Pogba and playing a beautiful through-ball to Raheem. He curled a cross to Wayne at the back post, who volleyed it in. *2–0!*

As Wayne threw his arms up in the air in triumph, Dele was the first to run over for a hug. They were international teammates now. England's experienced captain and England's exciting new star.

'Great work, Wazza!'

'Cheers, Dele – you started it, though. Well done!'

After that dream debut, surely Hodgson had to play Dele now?

CHAPTER 16

LOSING OUT TO LEICESTER

Dele was on fire, for club and country. The more Premier League games he played, the more brilliant he became.

A volley against Aston Villa,

Another one against West Brom,

And an even better one against Everton...

Away at Crystal Palace, Tottenham were drawing 1–1 with ten minutes to go. But only a win would do for Pochettino's team.

'Come on!' he urged his players on.

Dele got his manager's message. He pushed forward, looking for a way to win it. The Palace defence was getting deeper and deeper, so it would need to be something special.

Harry played a long pass to Christian, who nodded it down to Dele. Right what next? He was just outside the box, and as the ball arrived, he could see Mile Jedinak rushing towards him. Dele had to be quick and he had to be clever, just like during the old days at Heelands Courts.

Tap! He controlled it on the volley,

Flick! He lifted the ball over Jedinak's head,

Turn! He swung his body around, so that he was facing the target,

And *Shoot!* He blasted the ball into the bottom corner. *2–1!*

Gooooooooooooooooooooaaaaaaaaaaaaaaaalllllllllllll llllllllllllll!!!!!!!!!!!!!!!!!!!!

Wow, what a wondergoal! The whole of Selhurst Park was stunned – Palace *and* Tottenham, players *and* supporters. Well, everyone except Dele. He knew that he was capable of all kinds of magic.

'Get in, you hero!' Danny Rose screamed, jumping on his teammate's back.

Dele was the matchwinner, and who was there watching in the crowd? Hodgson, the England manager. The timing was perfect!

Just when other teams were falling apart, Tottenham were growing stronger. With an amazing win away at Manchester City, they jumped up from fourth place to second. Suddenly, anything seemed possible for Spurs, even winning the Premier League title!

First, however, they would have to catch the surprise league leaders, Leicester City. With nine games to go, the Foxes were five points clear at the top.

'We're going to have to win them all from now on!' Pochettino warned his players.

Nine wins in a row? That would be a very difficult task, but Dele was determined to do his best to achieve it.

He set up two goals for Harry against Aston Villa. *2–0!*

And then he set up another goal for Harry against Bournemouth. *3–0!*

Leicester's lead, however, was still five points, and it became seven when Tottenham drew at Liverpool. *Nooooo!* Dele's title dreams were fading fast, but he wasn't giving up. Spurs had to keep believing.

He scored their first goal against Manchester United. *3–0!*

And then he scored two more at Stoke City, including yet another volley. *4–0!*

Just days after his twentieth birthday, Dele was up to ten league goals for the season. The team win was the most important thing, however. And when Leicester drew with West Ham, that meant Tottenham were only five points behind again, with four games to go.

'Come on, we can catch them!' their captain Hugo spurred them on. 'The way we're playing this season, we don't deserve to finish second!'

West Brom at home didn't sound too tricky, but they were a well-organised team and they could be really hard to beat. If Tottenham could make an early breakthrough, though…

Harry played a one-two with Dele and then burst into the box. It looked certain to be goal number twenty-five for the striker, but somehow, he hit the post instead.

'Nooooo!' Dele groaned. He had been sure that Harry would score.

That was the start of a disappointing day for Tottenham, and for Dele in particular. Wherever he went on the pitch, West Brom's tough-tackling midfielder Claudio Yacob was right behind him. The Argentinian always tried to win the ball fairly, but he didn't mind fouling his opponent if he had to.

'Ref!' Dele complained, growing more and more frustrated.

Then in the twenty-sixth minute, for the first time in a Tottenham shirt, he really lost his cool. As Yacob chased back to stop him, Dele swung an arm into his stomach and gave him a sneaky kick.

Although the referee didn't see it, the rest of the world watching at home did. Soon, it was all over social media and Dele was in deep trouble. He played on for the rest of the match, but that turned out to be the end of his season. Afterwards, the FA charged him with violent conduct and handed him a three-game ban.

What a disaster! That meant Tottenham would have to take on Chelsea, Southampton and Newcastle without him. And after that bad draw against West Brom, they now needed to win all three.

At first, Dele was angry at Yacob. 'That's not fair – he fouled me first!'

But once he calmed down, he switched his anger to himself. 'How could I have been so stupid? You just can't react like that, no matter what. Man, I really let my team down!'

It was a horrible feeling that Dele would never forget. He apologised to all his Tottenham teammates and to his fans on Twitter:

'Gutted that my season is over. Will learn from this and come back stronger.'

However, he knew that words alone weren't enough. Dele would have to show he was sorry by becoming an even better player next season. Until then, all he could do was support his club from the sidelines.

'Come on, Spurs!'

Tottenham had to beat Chelsea, otherwise Leicester would be crowned Premier League Champions. At half-time, Dele's teammates seemed to be on track.

Érik slipped a pass through to Harry. *1–0!*

Christian slipped a pass through to Son. *2–0!*

'Yes, lads!' Dele shouted. So far so good.

But in the second half, Spurs lost their confidence and let Chelsea back into the game.

Gary Cahill scored from a goalmouth scramble. *2–1!*

'Uh oh,' Dele thought to himself. Suddenly, it didn't look good for Tottenham's title hopes.

With ten minutes to go, Eden Hazard played a one-two with Diego Costa, and then curled a shot into the top corner. *2–2!*

'Nooooooo!' Dele groaned in despair. All that effort all season long, and now Tottenham would have no trophy to show for it.

Dele was still so young, with lots to learn, and there was plenty of time left for him to win the Premier League title. But losing out to Leicester, and finishing second? No, he couldn't let that happen again.

CHAPTER 17

ANOTHER LEARNING EXPERIENCE AT EURO 2016

Fortunately, Dele didn't have long to dwell on his Premier League disappointment. Because in early June, he was off to France to play for England at Euro 2016. Yes, Dele had done it; he had earned a place in Hodgson's squad.

'Come on!' He celebrated with his fellow Tottenham teammates, Harry, Danny, Kyle and Eric. Together, they were going to make their country proud by finally bringing football home.

Was Dele, aged nineteen, really ready to become England's midfield maestro? Yes! He had followed up his fantastic goal against France with another great game against Germany. This time, he didn't score but he helped lead his team to an incredible comeback.

After sixty minutes in Berlin, England had been 2–0 down and facing a bad defeat. Dele didn't give up, though; he couldn't, not if he wanted to go to Euro 2016. So he kept working hard, running from box to box for his team. Once he had won the ball back, *ZOOM!* he raced forward to help Harry in attack. Dele could do it all; he was the complete midfielder.

Harry scored the first, before Jamie Vardy equalised with a beautiful flick finish. And then with seconds to go, Eric won it with a powerful header. *3–2 to England!*

What a win! The team had shown real strength and spirit. Surely, this was the side that should start at the Euros?

'If they are good enough, they are old enough,' the BBC declared, 'and Alli is good enough.'

The England manager agreed. 'It's an exciting, hungry and energetic bunch of players,' Hodgson said as he announced the twenty-three players that he was taking to France. His midfielders would be:

Adam Lallana,

James Milner,

Jack Wilshere,

Jordan Henderson,

Ross,

Eric,

And Dele!

Amazing, although Dele definitely wasn't going to the Euros to just sit on the bench and have a holiday in the sun. No, he was determined to secure his place in England's starting XI. He didn't mind where he played, just as long as he did play.

When it came to England's first Euro 2016 game against Russia, there he was, Number 20, walking out in his white shirt for kick-off.

It wasn't Dele's greatest game for England, but he still showed flashes of his bravery and brilliance. Every time his team attacked, he burst forward from central midfield to support the strikers. At the end of the first half, Dele found himself near the corner flag, surrounded by three Russian defenders, but he used his sublime skills to escape with the ball.

Olé!

When Eric scored a super free kick in the second half, it looked like England were off to an excellent start. But no, in injury time, Vasili Berezutski jumped the highest at the back post and headed home the equaliser. *1–1!*

'Noooo!' Dele groaned as he watched the ball cross the goal line. England deserved a lot more than a draw, but sometimes, football wasn't fair. It was another painful lesson for him to learn.

In their second match against Wales, England were drawing 1–1 again, and the ninety minutes were almost up. Two games, two points – that wasn't good enough. They really needed to win, otherwise it would put a lot of pressure on that final group game against Slovakia...

As Daniel Sturridge slid a pass through to Jamie, Dele made his move, bursting into the box.

'Yes!' he called out and Jamie played it straight away.

Dele's first touch was good but there were three Welsh players blocking his path to goal. Even he couldn't dance his way through that! So instead, he cleverly dragged the ball to his left, just as a defender dived in.

'Hey, penalty!' Dele cried out as he fell to the floor,
but the game carried on because his flick had fallen
to Daniel. *BANG!... GOAL! 2–1 to England!*

In a flash, Dele was back up on his feet and racing
towards the corner flag to celebrate their crucial goal.

'Get in!' he screamed, jumping up on Danny's
back as the England supporters in the stadium went
wild all around them.

Their Euro 2016 dream was still alive. A 0–0
draw against Slovakia was enough to take England
through to the Round of 16. Phew! There, they
would face Iceland, one of the surprise teams of
the tournament.

'Don't underestimate them!' Hodgson warned
his players. 'They're a strong side and this is the
knockouts now, so anything can happen.'

For the first few minutes of the match, it looked
like the England players had listened carefully to
their manager. Daniel curled a dangerous long ball
through to Raheem, who dribbled into the penalty
area and was fouled by the Iceland keeper. *Penalty!*
Wayne stepped up and scored from the spot. *1–0!*

What a start! After taking the lead, however, England switched off straight away.

Kári Árnason flicked on the long throw and Ragnar Sigurdsson slid in to score. *1–1!*

'Who was marking him?' Joe Hart yelled angrily at his defence. 'Wake up – we haven't won yet!'

Dele tried his best to get England back in front, but his swerving strike flew just over the crossbar.

'Ooooooooo!' Dele sighed deeply, putting his hands to his face. He was so close to scoring at Euro 2016.

England were looking exciting in attack, but dreadful in defence. Dele could only watch in horror as Gylfi Sigurdsson flicked it on to Jón Dadi Bödvarsson, who passed it across to Kolbeinn Sigthórsson.

'Close him down!' Dele cried out with every other England fan in the stadium.

But no, the defenders let the Iceland striker take one touch, then another, and then fire a shot that squirmed through Hart's gloves and over the goal line. *2–1!*

For a moment, the England players just stood

there, frozen in shock. What was going on? Although there was still plenty of time left, they just couldn't find a way to fight back.

Wayne's strikes flew wide,

Harry's headers landed safely in the goalkeeper's gloves,

Dele's scuffed shot looped up high over the bar,

And in the very last minute, Chris Smalling completely messed up his header.

Noooooooooo!

It just wasn't meant to be for England. At the final whistle, Dele dropped to his knees in despair. The team had failed big time, letting everyone down. After all those great expectations, it was such an embarrassing way to exit Euro 2016.

At the lowest point in their international careers, all the England players could do was learn from it and come back stronger. As Dele sat there in the six-yard box in Nice, he tried to think positively. He told himself the same thing that he had told himself after Tottenham's Premier League title disappointment:

'We can't let this happen again.'

CHAPTER 18

DELE THE DESTROYER

Dele's Euros experience did knock his confidence for a little while, but not for long. By Premier League Gameweek Four, he was back on the scoresheet for Spurs.

'Yesssss!' Dele cheered, raising his left arm to the fans who loved him and sang his name:

We've got Alli, Dele Alli
I just don't think you understand,
He only cost five mill,
He's better than Özil,
We've got Dele Alli!

Although Alli was still his surname, he now wore 'Dele' on the back of his shirt instead. That's who he was: Dele the Destroyer. He was back to his best, and so were Tottenham, challenging for the league title once again. Although many of the teams around them looked stronger now, Dele wasn't afraid of anyone.

Manchester City had brought in former Barcelona manager, Pep Guardiola, and spent over £140 million on new players. So what? When they came to White Hart Lane, Tottenham beat them 2–0, even without Harry. Late in the first half, Dele burst between the City centre-backs to reach Son's through-ball and then slid a shot past Claudio Bravo.

Gooooooooooooooooooooaaaaaaaaaaaaaaaaaalllllllllllll llllllllllllllll!!!!!!!!!!!!!!!!!!!!!!

'Come on!' Dele screamed, punching the air again and again.

Chelsea had brought in former Juventus manager, Antonio Conte, and spent nearly £120 million on new players. So what? When they came to White Hart Lane, Dele destroyed them. The Blues had stopped them from winning the 2015–16 title, and now he wanted revenge.

So as Christian looked up to cross the ball in, Dele

positioned himself perfectly, inside the box and in between two Chelsea defenders.

BOOM! He jumped up high, putting plenty of power on the header. The ball looped up and over Thibaut Courtois's desperate dive. 1–0!

Gooooooooooooooooooooaaaaaaaaaaaaaaaallllllllllllll llllllllllllll!!!!!!!!!!!!!!!!!!!!!

Dele was so delighted that he threw himself in amongst the Tottenham fans.

You legend!

We love you!

The yellow card was totally worth it for that amazing feeling.

Then, early in the second half, Dele did it again. This time, Christian's cross was higher and deeper, but the result was the same. *BOOM!*

Gooooooooooooooooooooaaaaaaaaaaaaaaaallllllllllllll llllllllllllll!!!!!!!!!!!!!!!!!!!!!

Dele saluted all the Spurs supporters on his way to the corner flag. It was celebration time.

'Come onnnnnnnnnnnnnn!'

Even with Harry back as Spurs' main striker, Dele

still couldn't stop scoring. That was his seventh goal in his last four games, and his tenth of the season. He had already equalled his last year's total and January had only just begun! Back in August, he had set himself a target of fifteen goals, but now he needed to aim even higher – twenty goals? Twenty-five?

'Hey, I'm the top-scorer at Tottenham, okay?' Harry joked as they did their special goal celebration handshake together.

'Well, we'll see about that!' Dele replied, giving his most mischievous grin.

Although they were very different characters, Harry and Dele had three important things in common:

1) They always wanted to win,

2) They loved playing PlayStation,

And most important of all,

3) They loved playing football!

Especially together, in the same Tottenham and England teams. They had a special connection and they always seemed to know where each other would be on the pitch. Before every game, Harry and

Dele discussed their opponents and worked out ways to destroy them.

Harry passed to Dele just outside the West Brom box and then carried on his run, calling for the one-two. But how? Dele had two tall defenders right in front of him! As always, however, he found a quick, clever way out of a tricky situation. He scooped the ball just over their heads and as it dropped down, Harry was there to volley it in. *4–0!*

Another awesome assist for Dele and another hat-trick for Harry! Thanks to their deadly duo, Tottenham were back up to second place in the Premier League table, seven points behind the leaders, Chelsea.

'Not this again!' the Spurs supporters thought to themselves. Last season, they had lost out to Leicester; were they going to lose out to Chelsea this time?

Dele did his very best to create a different ending to the story.

He headed Tottenham back into the game against Manchester City. *GOAL!*

And he scored the winner against Everton with a clever flick. *GOAL!*

Then, when Harry had to miss another four games through injury, Dele stepped forward to become Spurs' big game player again. Even at such a young age, his club could rely on him.

He scored the winner against Southampton from the penalty spot. *GOAL!*

And he set up Son to secure the victory against Burnley. *ASSIST!*

Away at Swansea, Spurs found themselves 1–0 down with six minutes to go. Uh oh, even a draw wouldn't do, not if they wanted to catch Chelsea at the top. As always, Dele desperately wanted to win, and so he pulled up his socks and pressed the 'destroy' button.

Christian's shot pinballed its way through the Swansea box, until it reached Dele, who was all alone at the back post. *1–1!*

'Come on!' he urged his teammates as they ran back for the restart. There was still time for another Tottenham goal... or two.

Son raced through and shot past the keeper. *2–1!*

And then in the final seconds, Dele slid a perfect pass through to Christian, who finished things off. *3–1!*

What a comeback, and again it was Dele who had made the difference! With sixteen goals and seven assists in only his second season in the Premier League, he was well on his way to becoming a world-class player.

But what Dele wanted most was to lift the league title. Tottenham kept on winning, and at last, Chelsea were beaten, by Manchester United. The gap was now just four points, with five games to go. And next up for Spurs? The North London derby against Arsenal.

'It's time to show them that we're the best team in this city!' Dele declared confidently before kick-off.

There was a noisy, nervous atmosphere at White Hart Lane as the players walked out onto the pitch. Tottenham absolutely had to win; they couldn't let their bitter rivals ruin their chances of becoming Premier League Champions. No way!

Early in the second half, Dele dribbled into the

Arsenal penalty area, before cutting the ball back to Christian. His shot was blocked by the keeper, but what about the rebound?

Dele reacted first, even faster than the four Arsenal defenders who were much closer to the bouncing ball. He desperately wanted to win, and with a big, brave stretch of his left leg, he kicked it in. *1–0!*

Goooooooooooooooooooaaaaaaaaaaaaaaaaallllllllllll llllllllllllll!!!!!!!!!!!!!!!!!!!!!

Dele had done it! And three minutes later, Harry made it 2–0. Thanks to their deadly duo, Tottenham were still in the title race.

But sadly, not for much longer. A week later, they suffered a surprise 1–0 defeat at West Ham. And with a 1–0 win at West Brom, Chelsea were crowned Premier League Champions.

For Dele, it was another frustrating 'nearly' season. He finished with twenty-two goals and thirteen assists in all competitions, plus a second PFA Young Player of the Year award in a row. He was making huge progress as a player, but there was still one major thing missing – a team trophy with Tottenham.

CHAPTER 19

BIG GOALS AGAINST THE BEST

1 November 2017, Wembley Stadium

Playing in the Champions League – that was the dream for so many football-mad kids, including Dele. As a boy, he had loved watching the tournament on TV: the glamorous European giants, the competitive clashes and, of course, the amazing anthem. Dele didn't really like classical music, but 'Zadok the Priest' was brilliant! Hearing it brought back so many special memories.

Now, Dele was lucky enough to be living out his dream. He still found it hard to believe. His Tottenham team were about to take on Real Madrid at Wembley in the greatest club competition in the world. And if they won, they would make it through to the Last 16.

Come on you Spurs!

Dele's first year of Champions League football had been a disappointing one. Although he had scored in the last group game against CSKA Moscow, Tottenham had been knocked out and thrown into the Europa League instead. There, things had got even worse, especially for Dele. He was sent off for a reckless, late tackle against Gent, which meant he had to miss the first three Champions League matches of the next season:

Borussia Dortmund at home,

APOEL Nicosia away,

And Real Madrid away.

But at last, Dele was back, and just in time to face Real Madrid at home. 'His best form is coming' – that's what his manager Pochettino had recently said about him. Well, this was the perfect time for Dele to prove it.

Wow, what a match-up it was going to be: Dele,

Harry and Christian versus four-time Ballon d'Or winner Cristiano Ronaldo, Karim Benzema and Isco.

As the anthem played, however, Dele didn't seem nervous at all. No, he stood there calmly stretching his neck and imagining the great goals he was going to score. To make it to the very top, he had to believe in his own ability. He played football without fear, whether he was in the park with his mates or taking on Ronaldo and Real Madrid at Wembley.

Right from the kick-off, Dele raced around the field, battling hard for every ball. This time, there were no cheeky nutmegs on Modrić; he was a more mature player now and winning was all that mattered. Every time he got the ball, Dele carried it forward, looking to link up with Harry.

Harry wasn't Tottenham's only fantastic finisher, though. Dele was a dangerous goal scorer too. As Kieran Trippier crossed from the right, he was the only Spurs forward in the box, with Real Madrid defenders all around him. It looked like an easy catch for the keeper, but Dele wanted to

win so badly that he refused to lose the battle. He
outmuscled Nacho and managed to poke the ball
past Kiko Casilla. *1–0!*

*Goooooooooooooooooooooaaaaaaaaaaaaaaaalllllllllllll
lllllllllllllll!!!!!!!!!!!!!!!!!!!!!*

What a way to return to Champions League
action, with a goal against Real Madrid! Dele raced
over to the Spurs supporters, with Kieran and Harry
right behind him.

'Come on!' they roared together.

After that, Dele's confidence was sky-high. He
even played another of his scoop passes before half-
time, lifting the ball over the top of the Real defence,
but Harry's volley flew straight at the keeper.

'Man, you're on fire!' Harry smiled, giving a big
thumbs-up.

Even Ronaldo couldn't ruin Dele's night. The
Portuguese striker did eventually score, but it was
game over by then.

Just as Real Madrid started to dominate the game,
Dele got the ball and dribbled at Casemiro. With a
drop of his left shoulder, he beat the Brazilian once,

and then when Casemiro came back for a slide
tackle, Dele skipped past him again.

Olé!

He was into the Real Madrid box now, with
just Sergio Ramos in front of him. *BANG!* Dele's
shot deflected off Ramos, giving the goalkeeper no
chance. *2–0!*

*Goooooooooooooooooooooaaaaaaaaaaaaaaaalllllllllllll
llllllllllllll!!!!!!!!!!!!!!!!!!!*

Dele was enjoying the best night of his life, in
front of over 80,000 fans at Wembley. He leapt up,
punching the air like a prize-winning boxer. What
a feeling! Tottenham were beating the twelve-time
European Champions and he had scored both of
the goals.

With the confidence surging through his body,
Dele decided to try a cheeky nutmeg on Ramos. He
couldn't help himself, and it worked!

Olé!

The Real Madrid captain didn't know how to
handle such speed and skill. Soon, Dele launched
another counter-attack, strolling past Ramos with

ease. Near the halfway line, he poked the ball forward to Harry, who then passed it through to Christian. *3–0!*

Unbelievable! As Christian slid across the Wembley grass on his knees, Harry and Dele rushed over to join him, followed by the rest of the team. Together, Tottenham were thrashing Real Madrid!

Dele even had a glorious opportunity to complete his hat-trick. With fifteen minutes to go, Kieran delivered another incredible cross from the right, which dropped down right onto Dele's head. He was unmarked in the middle and just six yards out – he had to score, surely? But no, somehow, he glanced it wide.

'Noooooooo!' Dele groaned, covering his face with his hands and then slapping the crossbar in frustration.

So nearly 4–0! That would have been the perfect end to a perfect night. But never mind, Dele kept battling all the way until the final whistle.

'Get in!' he yelled with his last lungful of energy.

What a performance – they were through to the

Last 16! It was hugs and celebration handshakes all round for Tottenham's Champions League heroes. However, there was no question about who their man of the match was: Dele!

He wasn't having his most successful season in the Premier League so far, but on his Champions League comeback, Dele had just scored two big goals against the best team around. Nothing fazed him, not even going head-to-head with Ronaldo. With him, Harry and Christian in attack, Tottenham were capable of achieving anything.

'We don't want to only compete with these top teams,' Dele told the journalists afterwards, the sweat still shining on his calmly focused face. 'We want to be beating them.'

CHAPTER 20

WORLD CUP 2018

Dele had been waiting a long time for the summer of 2018. Why? Because it was a World Cup summer! Growing up, those were some of his happiest memories. Dele loved everything about the tournament: the barbeques, the sense of optimism, the England flags everywhere, and of course, the football itself.

This time, however, he wouldn't be at home, watching on TV with the Hickfords, like in 2010 and 2014. No, he would be out on the pitch, playing for his country!

England announced their 2018 World Cup squad

with a special video, where each player's name was revealed one by one. Raheem was first, then John Stones, then Trent Alexander-Arnold…

Eventually, three excited teenagers appeared on screen, huddled around the centre-circle of an artificial football pitch that was similar to the one at Heelands Courts.

'DELE ALLI,' they cheered, bouncing up and down together. 'OI OI OI!'

Soon, Dele's family and friends were bouncing up and down too.

'Congratulations, we're so proud of you!' cried Alan and Sally.

'Nice one, bro – I knew you could do it,' Harry said, giving him a hug. After his own football career had been ended by injury, he was now Dele's agent as well as his best friend. 'Right, we better pack our bags – Russia, here we come!'

A lot had changed for England since their Euro 2016 disaster. First of all, Roy Hodgson had been replaced as manager by Sam Allardyce and then by Dele's old Under-21 manager, Gareth Southgate.

As a former England international himself, Southgate understood the nation's expectations and he had big plans for the future: 'I'm determined to give the country a team that they're proud of and one that they're going to enjoy watching play and develop.'

Dele liked the sound of that, and he liked working with Southgate. He was building an exciting new England squad and Dele wanted to be a big part of it, starting with the 2018 World Cup.

'It's an honour to be named in the England squad for the World Cup,' he posted on social media alongside two photos: one of him boarding the team plane and the other of him back in his early international days with the Under-17s. 'It's a dream come true! Get me to Russia!!!'

Dele and his teammates were determined to move on from the painful memories of Euro 2016 and give the country something to cheer about.

Ahead of the tournament, Southgate had switched the England formation from a 4-3-3 to a 3-5-2 with attacking wing-backs. It was new for some, but not for Dele. He had played in that formation many times at Tottenham, under Pochettino. With Kieran and Danny flying down the flanks, Dele's role was to run box-to-box through the middle, getting back to win the ball and then forward to help Harry up front. That's how they had thrashed the mighty Real Madrid, so would it work for England too?

'Of course, it will!' Dele declared confidently as the team walked out for their first group game against Tunisia. Southgate had created a great squad spirit, where everyone got on well and knew their roles. With Jordan Henderson sitting deeper in defensive midfield, Dele and Jesse Lingard had the freedom to attack as much as possible.

In only the second minute of the match, Dele raced onto Jordan's long pass and looked to pick out Raheem in the middle. The Tunisia centre-back blocked the cross, but Dele got a second go. He poked it across to Jesse, whose shot was saved by the keeper.

So close already! Jesse stood there with his hands

to his mouth, and Dele with his hands on his head. What an amazing start that would have been...

'Keep going – the goal is coming!' Harry, their captain, clapped and cheered.

Just seven minutes later, it arrived. The Tunisia keeper managed to stop John's thunderous header, but the rebound fell to Harry, who hardly ever missed. *1–0 to England!*

'Get in!' Dele yelled out as he joined the player pile-on.

England were on top and they soon had chances to make it 2–0. Kieran's cross whistled through the gap between Dele and Harry, and then Jordan's long-range rocket flew straight at the keeper.

The Three Lions were attacking with such style and confidence, but out of the blue, they conceded a penalty. *1–1!* Although the equaliser came as a shock for England, they still had plenty of time left to score a winner...

But Dele's clever flick header was cleared off the line,

Then Jesse hit the post,

And then the referee refused to give a penalty when Harry was clearly fouled.

Uh oh – were England heading for another disappointing draw? Dele ran and ran but with ten minutes to go, he had to come off. He had picked up an injury in the first half, and the pain was getting worse.

Instead, it was Harry who was England's hero yet again. With a swing of his strong neck, he powered the ball into the net. *2–1!*

'Yesssss!' Dele shouted on the sidelines with the rest of the squad. *Phew!* It hadn't been easy, but in the end, England had that first World Cup win that they were looking for.

On to the next game, but would Dele be able to play against Panama? 'Frustrating to have picked up a slight injury on Monday,' he posted on Twitter. 'Will do everything in my power to get back to full fitness asap!'

England didn't need Dele for that game anyway. He watched from the bench as the goals went flying in. *1–0, 2–0, 3–0... 6–1!*

'Man, I would definitely have scored today!' he joked with Harry, who had bagged a hat-trick.

Oh well, Dele's first World Cup goal would just have to wait. After resting for the final group game against Belgium, he came back for England's Round of 16 clash with Colombia.

In a fierce and fiery match, Dele managed to last the first eighty minutes. As he trudged off the field, England were 1–0 up and on their way to the quarter-finals. But deep in injury time, disaster struck. Yerry Mina scored from a corner, and the game went to extra-time and then... PENALTIES!

For Dele, it was so difficult to watch. He wanted to be out there with his teammates on the halfway line, and then stepping up to score for England. Instead, however, he had to watch helplessly from the sidelines.

'Go on!' he muttered as Harry and Marcus Rashford made it two out of two.

'Noooo!' he groaned when Jordan missed.

'Yessss!' he cheered when Mateus Uribe missed too.

After that, it was all good news:

Kieran scored, then Jordan Pickford saved from Carlos Bacca, and then Eric stepped up to score the winner. England were through to the World Cup quarter-finals!

'Come on!' Dele roared as he raced over to join in the joyful celebrations. The pile of players was already pretty high, but he still jumped on the top.

Not only had England won, but they had won A PENALTY SHOOT-OUT! It was the first time that had happened in twenty-two years, and it filled the fans with hope and confidence.

The players, however, were taking it one step at a time. First, they needed to beat Sweden to book their place in the semi-finals.

It was Harry who gave them the lead, but not Harry Kane; no, Harry Maguire, their big centre-back with a head as hard as stone. *BOOM! 1–0!*

For the next twenty minutes, England's lead looked comfortable, but they really didn't want a repeat of the Tunisia game. A second goal would really help to settle things down...

As Jesse curled a cross into the box, Dele made
his move at the back post, racing in behind his
marker's back. The ball was coming straight
towards him; he wouldn't get a better chance than
this. How many times had he scored headers like
this for Tottenham? Loads! Dele jumped up high,
pushing his head towards the ball with power.
BOOM! It flew past the keeper before he could
really react. *2–0!*

*Gooooooooooooooooooooaaaaaaaaaaaaaaaaallllllllllll
lllllllllllllllll!!!!!!!!!!!!!!!!!!!!!*

Only once the ball had dropped down into the
net, did Dele allow himself to celebrate.

'YESSSSSSS!' he exploded with emotion.

Despite his injury problems, Dele had fought his
way back into the team and now, he had done it. He
had scored his first World Cup goal.

'Wow! World Cup semi-finals,' Dele wrote on
social media. 'Let's go, England!'

The next day, the players watched the videos of
all the amazing celebrations back home. They had
already given their country lots to cheer about in

Russia, but what if they could return with the World Cup trophy? They would be heroes forever!

Once more, Dele dared to dream. There were no nerves or doubts; he prepared like it was just a normal game, rather than a World Cup semi-final. In the England dressing room in Moscow, he went through the same old routine:

Right sock, then right boot (size 10), then right shin pad (the same ones he had worn since he was eleven years old),

Left sock, then left boot (size 10-and-a-half), then left shin pad...

Right, ready!

In the fourth minute against Croatia, Dele collected Jesse's pass and drove forward towards goal, until he was fouled by his old Real Madrid opponent, Modrić. *Free kick to England!* The position was perfect for a curler from Kieran. *1–0!*

'Yes, Tripps, you legend!' Dele cried out as he chased after his Tottenham teammate. England were on their way to the World Cup Final!

It was the perfect start and before half-time,

Harry had two glorious chances to make it 2–0. Unfortunately, he missed them both and as the second half went on, Croatia came back into the game. In the sixty-eighth minute, Šime Vrsaljko's cross flew all the way through to Ivan Perišić. *1–1!*

As the goal went in, Dele's heart sank. After all that running, after all that defending. His energy was gone; he was exhausted. He didn't give up, and England battled on into extra-time, but it was Croatia who grabbed the winning goal and a place in the World Cup Final.

At the final whistle, Dele dropped to the grass. He was absolutely devastated. He had never known a feeling like it – disappointment, rage, regret and pride all rolled into one. It was gutting to get so close to the final. The players had given everything, but it just wasn't quite enough. However, although they hadn't brought the World Cup home, they *had* brought football home. England had fallen in love with its national team once more.

Once he'd had a bit of time to calm down and think, Dele wrote a message to his social media followers:

'I want to thank everyone for the support we've received. This is going to take a while to get over, but I truly believe this team has a bright future and we will make England proud again!'

CHAPTER 21

EUROPEAN EXCITEMENT

'Back to work,' Dele posted on Twitter as he returned to Tottenham for preseason training. After a relaxing holiday, he was now ready to put his World Cup woes behind him and focus on club football again. Dele had a team trophy to try and win.

Second, second, third – for each of the last three years, Spurs had come so close to lifting the Premier League title. They had also reached two FA Cup semi-finals, but sadly, there was still no silverware to show for all their success. And if Spurs didn't win something soon, then their star players – Harry, Christian, Son – might move on to other clubs...

And, of course, Dele, might do the same. At the

age of twenty-two, he had already led a very eventful life, but he was about to set out on his most exciting adventure yet.

It only took Dele eighteen minutes to score his first goal of the 2018–19 season. As Serge Aurier looked up to cross the ball into the Newcastle box, he spotted Dele racing in at the back post, waving his arm frantically. It was a classic team move, but it seemed to work every time.

PING! Serge's cross was perfect, and Dele did the rest. He sprang up to meet the ball and nodded it down into the bottom corner.

Goooooooooooooooooooaaaaaaaaaaaaaaaaaallllllllllllll llllllllllllll!!!!!!!!!!!!!!!!!!!!

After a quick hug with Harry, he turned to the crowd and raised his right hand to his right eye, flipping it around to make a funny salute.

New season, new celebration, but same old super Dele.

As with most exciting adventures, however, there were also moments of misfortune. Dele hurt his hamstring while playing for England in September and had to miss four Premier League games, plus three crucial European ties:

Inter Milan 2 Tottenham 1,

Tottenham 2 Barcelona 4,

PSV Eindhoven 2 Tottenham 2...

Only one point from three games – uh oh, halfway through the group stage, it looked like Spurs' Champions League campaign was already over.

But when Dele came back, he helped to turn things around for his team.

...Tottenham 2 PSV Eindhoven 1,

Tottenham 1 Inter Milan 0...

With time running out, Moussa Sissoko dribbled the ball forward from midfield, and all the way into the Inter box.

'Yes!' Dele called out for it on the edge of the area.

When the pass arrived, it was slightly behind him. So rather than shoot for goal himself, Dele spun quickly and passed the ball into Christian's path. *1–0!*

'Yessss!' the two Tottenham players yelled at each other.

What an important goal, to keep their
Champions League hopes alive! Now, they just
needed to win their final group game, and they
would be through to the Last 16. The only problem:
the team they had to beat was Barcelona... away
at the Nou Camp.

That was going to be tough, but Dele was
always up for a challenge. He had already helped
Tottenham to thrash Ronaldo's Real Madrid, so why
not Lionel Messi's Barcelona too? They had
to believe.

But even Dele had a few doubts, when Ousmane
Dembélé raced through to score after only seven
minutes. Oh dear, Tottenham's tough task had just
got even tougher.

There was plenty of time left though, and over
in Italy, PSV had just taken the lead. *Phew!* If Inter
lost too, then Spurs could still go through.

That all changed, however, when Mauro Icardi
scored for Inter midway through the second half.
Suddenly, they jumped up into second place. So,
what could Tottenham do to fight back?

Although Dele wasn't having his greatest game, he never gave up, and neither did his teammates. With five minutes to go, Christian passed it to Érik, who passed it to Harry, who crossed it to Lucas Moura. *1–1!*

'Get in!' Together, Tottenham had grabbed the goal that they needed. But would that be enough? Yes! Over in Italy, Inter could only draw with PSV. Somehow, Spurs had pulled off the impossible – they were through to the Champions League Last 16!

Dele celebrated by helping to destroy Arsenal in the North London derby a week later. Away at the Emirates, he created Tottenham's first goal with a beautiful chipped pass to Son. *1–0!*

Then, early in the second half, Harry played a similar pass to Dele, who was through one-on-one with the Arsenal keeper. Could he score? Of course he could – and he did it in style. With the outside of his right boot, Dele dinked the ball over Petr Čech and into the bottom corner. *2–0!*

Gooooooooooooooooooooaaaaaaaaaaaaaaaallllllllllll llllllllllllll!!!!!!!!!!!!!!!!!!!!

Wow, what a finish!

Nothing could ruin Dele's big North London derby,
not even being hit on the head by a bottle. At first,
Dele turned around angrily to shout up into the
stand, but then he changed his mind. That would
only make things worse. So instead, he swapped his
glare for a mischievous grin raising two fingers on
one hand and making a zero with the other: 2–0
– just in case the Arsenal supporters had forgotten
what the score was.

It was so far so good for Dele's season, but sadly,
by the time the Champions League returned in
February, he was injured again. It was another
thigh strain and it meant he had to miss both
legs of Tottenham's tie with Borussia Dortmund.
Fortunately, they won it 4–0 even without him.

'Sorry mate, I don't think we need you anymore,'
Harry said afterwards. 'Nah, just joking! You'll be
back for the quarter-finals, right?'

'Try stopping me!' Dele replied.

In the Champions League quarter-finals, Spurs
were up against their Premier League rivals,

Manchester City, and it would be their first big European night at their brand-new, 60,000-seater stadium.

They won 1–0 at the Tottenham Hotspur Stadium, thanks to a penalty save from Hugo and a great goal from Son. Now, Spurs just had to stay strong at the Etihad.

'Bring it on!' cheered Dele, but it turned out to be the craziest football match he had ever played in.

First, Raheem curled a shot into the bottom corner. *1–1 on aggregate!*

Then Dele's through-ball to Christian was cut out, but the rebound fell to Son. *2–1 to Spurs!*

Then Christian passed to Son, who scored again. *3–1!*

Then Bernardo Silva's shot deflected in off Danny. *3–2!*

And finally, Raheem raced in at the back post to make it 3–3!

Five goals in only twenty-one minutes – what on earth was going on? Things did calm down after that. A whole thirty-eight minutes passed before the next goal, although unfortunately, it was Sergio Agüero who got it. *4–3 to City!*

Could Tottenham come back again? Yes, and in the strangest way! Kieran's corner-kick bounced off Fernando Llorente's hip and into the City net. After a quick VAR check, the goal was given: *4–4!*

'Come on!' the Tottenham players cheered, standing together in front of their fans.

As if that wasn't enough European excitement for one night, there was still one more twist in the tale. In injury time, Bernardo Silva intercepted Christian's pass and flicked it forward to Agüero, who squared it to Raheem, who fired a shot past Hugo. *5–4 to City!*

'Noooooo!' Dele growled as he watched from near the halfway line. Not another devastating defeat...

But wait! VAR was checking the goal again. And after what felt like hours of agony for Dele, the referee finally made his decision:

Agüero was offside – no goal!

Unbelievable scenes! Now, if Tottenham could just hold on for three more minutes, they would go through on away goals. It felt like forever, but they held on – and they were through.

'Yes, yes, yes!' Dele screamed, as he raced around the pitch hugging and high fiving everyone he saw. It felt too good to be true.

The Tottenham team formed a line and took a bow in front of their supporters, but it was only later that their incredible achievement really sank in. Somehow, despite all the drama along the way, Spurs were still in the Champions League, and Dele wanted the whole world to know it:

'UNREAL NIGHT!! WE'RE IN THE SEMIS!!'

CHAPTER 22

CHAMPIONS LEAGUE HIGHS AND LOWS

For the first leg of their Champions League semi-final against Ajax, the Tottenham team were without four of their star players:

The two Harrys – Kane and Winks,

Érik,

And Son.

Wow, they were missing a lot of goals and creativity in attack! Oh well, Spurs would just have to rely on their strong team spirit and their stars who were available:

Christian,

Lucas,

Hugo,

And, of course, Dele. With the pressure on, could he step up and become Tottenham's big game player once again?

Not in the first leg at the new White Hart Lane, unfortunately. As the teams walked out onto the pitch, Dele looked at the inspiring sight to his right. The Tottenham fans had formed a wall of white and blue, displaying the words, 'DARE TO DO'. That was their message to the players, but sadly even a deafening euphoric home crowd couldn't save Spurs from a disappointing defeat.

In the fifteenth minute, Hakim Ziyech slipped a perfect pass through to Donny van de Beek. *1–0 to Ajax!*

And that's how it stayed, despite Dele's best efforts. His first shot from the edge of the area was blocked by a defender and then he fired a volley straight at the Ajax keeper.

'Arggh!' Dele snarled, kicking the air in frustration. Harry would have scored it and he knew it.

Early in the second half, the scene looked set for a Kieran-to-Dele classic. But as the ball looped towards

him at the back post, Dele couldn't jump high
enough to head it down.

'Nooooooo!'

A 1–0 home defeat – it didn't look good, but
it wasn't a total disaster for Tottenham. Dele still
believed; they had battled back before to make it out
of Group B and then past Manchester City. Their best
chance of winning the Champions League wasn't
over yet.

Son and Érik were back for the second leg in
Amsterdam, but Spurs were still without the two
Harrys. Calm and focus would be key, plus goals,
of course. Dele knew that he would have to do better
this time, especially in attack. He had to
make the difference.

'Come on, we can do this!'

By half-time, however, it really did look like
game over. Ajax were 2–0 up on the night, and
3–0 up on aggregate. To make it to the Champions
League Final, Tottenham would have to score
three now.

'The next goal is going to be crucial,' Pochettino

told his players in the dressing room. 'If we score it, it's game on!'

Challenge accepted! Dele never even thought about giving up. Instead, he clenched his fists with determination. Tottenham had come too far in the tournament to get knocked out without a fight. Dele was desperate to win his first team trophy at the club, and this was their last chance of the season. There were forty-five minutes left and they had to give it everything.

Early in the second half, Danny played a long pass up to Lucas, who flicked it on to Dele as he entered the Ajax half. As he dribbled towards the penalty area, Dele twisted and turned his way past Frenkie de Jong, before threading a beautiful pass through to Lucas. *3–1!*

Tottenham had scored the next goal – it was game on! As Dele ran back for the restart, he could feel the belief returning all around him. They could do this; they could pull off their most incredible comeback ever. They just needed two more goals now...

Spurs were on the attack, with their confidence back. Kieran delivered a dangerous cross to Fernando, who looked certain to score from three yards out. Somehow, however, the Ajax keeper saved it.

Nooooo, what a wasted opportunity!

But wait! The ball spilled out to Lucas, who weaved his way through the crowded box, turned and curled an unstoppable left-foot strike into the bottom corner. *3–2!*

Woah, Tottenham now only needed one more goal to win it. Was it going to be their night, after all?

'Go on!' Pochettino urged his team forward.

The last fifteen minutes were full of end-to-end drama.

Ziyech hit the post for Ajax,

Then Jan headed the ball against the bar.

Was that it – Tottenham's last chance? No, in the final seconds of injury time, Fernando knocked a long ball down to Dele, on the edge of the 'D'. There was no time to think; it was all about instinct now.

Dele had spotted a bit of space in between the Ajax defence, and so with a quick swivel of his body and a delicate flick of his right foot, he placed the pass right there...

ZOOM! Lucas was onto it, beating Matthijs de Ligt to the ball...

'Finish it, finish it!' Dele muttered as he watched.

...And with another swing of his left foot, Lucas found the bottom corner with the last kick of the game. *3–3!*

Their incredible comeback was complete! As the Ajax players collapsed to the grass, the Tottenham team went wild. Against all the odds, they had done it – they were into the Champions League Final!

It all felt like a dream to Dele. Had that really just happened? Yes, it had, and he had helped make a difference! Lucas was Tottenham's hat-trick hero, but it was Dele's quick thinking that had created his winning goal.

The celebrations went on and on, moving from the pitch to the dressing room, where the music played, and the champagne sprayed. None of the Tottenham players wanted their magical moment to end. It was hard to describe the feeling, but Dele did his best:

'BEST NIGHT OF MY LIFE!! MADRID HERE WE COME!!'

However, after that Champions League high came a Champions League low. After only two minutes of the final in Madrid, Tottenham were losing 1–0 to Liverpool.

Sadio Mané burst into the box and his pass bounced off Moussa's arm. *Penalty!*

'No way!' Dele thought, stopping still on the edge of the area. He couldn't watch as Mohamed Salah scored from the spot.

It was the worst possible start for Tottenham, and this time, they couldn't turn things around. As hard as he tried, Dele couldn't get into the game. His touch was heavy, and he was missing easy tackles. What was going on? He was meant to be a big game player, and this was the biggest game of all!

When Dele did finally get a chance to shoot, he chipped the ball so high that Alisson had an easy catch to make.

'Ohhhh!' Dele sighed as his shoulders slumped. Although it wasn't an easy chance, he still expected better of himself. So, what else could he do to make a difference for his team? He had to keep trying.

Dele played a slick pass to Son to set up a quick counter-attack, but Virgil van Dijk was there to deal with the danger.

Dele burst in at the back post to meet Kieran's cross, but the ball was a little too high, and so was his header.

Dele set up Son again, but Alisson dived down to save his shot.

No, this time it just wasn't to be for Tottenham. And in the eighty-first minute, Dele's night came to an early end. When he saw his number, '20', flash up on the electronic subs board, he couldn't believe it. What?! Why was Pochettino taking him off, just when he was getting into the game? As he stormed off the field, Dele was so furious that he threw his drinks bottle against the back of the dug-out. *THUD!*

While Dele sat there sulking on the bench, Divock Origi made it 2–0 to Liverpool. Game over, and Tottenham's dream of winning the Champions League trophy over.

Dele did go up to collect his runners-up medal, but he wasn't going to wear it proudly around his neck. That would have to wait, until he eventually won the competition.

'I'm heartbroken,' Dele admitted honestly in the press conference afterwards. 'It's been an amazing journey for us as a team, but now, we need to take this painful feeling and use it to drive us on next season.'

CHAPTER 23

NEW MOTIVATION FROM MOURINHO

During his summer break of 2019, Dele thought long and hard about that painful loss to Liverpool, and about his future too. Although he was proud to be part of such a successful Tottenham team, he couldn't help feeling a bit frustrated. Were they ever going to win something? Semi-finalists in the FA Cup *and* the League Cup; runners-up in the Premier League (twice) *and* the Champions League. Each year, they worked so hard to get so close to a trophy.

Dele tried his best to ignore the comments on social media, but he knew what people were saying:

'They'll never win anything – that's Spurs for you!'

'Kane, Alli, Pochettino – they're good but you

can't call them great. I mean, where are their
trophies?'

It was now or never for Spurs as the 2019–20
season kicked off. They couldn't keep finishing
second forever, especially not now that they had
strengthened the squad by spending £80 million
on French midfielder Tanguy Ndombele and young
English winger Ryan Sessegnon.

But after eight Premier League matches, Tottenham
found themselves way down in ninth position, and
Dele had only played a total of thirty minutes. For the
first few games, he had been injured, but once he got
fit again, Pochettino left him on the bench.

'What's going on?' he wondered as Spurs lost 3–0
to Brighton without him. 'What did I do wrong?'

Their results were even worse in the Champions
League. After a 2–2 draw with Olympiakos, Bayern
Munich thrashed them 7–2 at the Tottenham
Hotspur Stadium. How humiliating! Just four months
after reaching the Champions League Final, they
were falling apart.

Something had to change and that something turned

out to be the manager. After five league games without a win, Daniel Levy decided to sack Pochettino.

Dele couldn't believe it; after everything they'd been through together! 'I can't thank this man enough,' he posted on Twitter. 'He's taught me so much and I'm so grateful for everything he's done for me.'

Now, though, it was time for a fresh start. The next day, Spurs announced the new man in charge: José Mourinho.

The Portuguese manager wasn't the most popular choice, but he certainly had a record for winning. He had won three Premier league titles with Chelsea, plus two Champions League trophies with Porto and Inter Milan. And he was famous for getting the best out of his players, including one of Dele's childhood heroes: Frank Lampard.

Growing up, Dele wanted to be just like Lampard and Gerrard – box-to-box midfielders who scored lots of goals and played with such drive and determination. So, maybe Mourinho could help him to find his best form again...

'Are you Dele Alli or are you his brother?' his
new manager asked him at one of their first training
sessions together.

What?! What was this guy talking about?

'I'm Dele,' he replied. 'Obviously.'

'Okay, good – then I need you to play like Dele,'
his manager told him, 'like you did in your first two
seasons at Tottenham.'

Mourinho wanted Dele to go back to doing what he
did best – attacking. For the last few years, Pochettino
had played him in a slightly deeper midfield role,
but now he was being asked to become a Number
10 again. Goals and assists – that's what his team
needed from him. So, with that extra motivation from
Mourinho, Dele set out to rediscover his best form.

Against West Ham, he set up the first goal for Son,
with a simple turn and pass. *1–0!*

Then, after slipping over, he skilfully managed to
flick another pass through to Son, while he was still
down on the floor.

Olé!

Dele's quick, clever thinking had returned. Son

raced down the wing and crossed it into Lucas. *2–0!*

'That was the real Dele,' Mourinho declared happily after his first match as manager.

That strong start didn't last long, however. Three days later in the Champions League, Tottenham went 2–0 down at home against Olympiakos. If they lost, they might not make it through the group stage. But just before half-time, a determined Dele helped lead another incredible Spurs comeback.

As the Olympiakos centre-back went to clear away Serge's cross, he completely missed his kick! The ball whistled through the six-yard box until it reached Dele, who had snuck in between two defenders, like he always loved to do. *2–1!*

Goooooooooooooooooooaaaaaaaaaaaaaaaaalllllllllllllllllllllllll!!!!!!!!!!!!!!!!!!!!

'Come on!' Dele urged his teammates. 'It's not over yet!'

From a quick throw-in, Lucas set up Harry. *2–2!*

Dele tricked his way into the box and then crossed the ball into the danger zone. Son got the flick-on and Serge finished it off beautifully. *3–2!*

And Dele wasn't done yet. A minute later, he
dribbled the ball all the way down the left wing, from
deep inside his own half. He tried to shrug off the
Olympiakos defender, but he fouled him eventually.
Free kick! Christian curled it in, and Harry headed it
home. *4–2!*

'Champions League Last 16, here we come!'
Tottenham's attacking trio celebrated together.

In his first two games under Mourinho, Dele had
won two man of the match awards, and the key
moments kept on coming. Against Bournemouth,
Dele made two of his trademark runs, on both
occasions bursting into the box and finding the net:

*Goooooooooooooooooooaaaaaaaaaaaaaaaalllllllllllll
lllllllllllllll!!!!!!!!!!!!!!!!!!!*

*Goooooooooooooooooooaaaaaaaaaaaaaaaalllllllllllll
lllllllllllllll!!!!!!!!!!!!!!!!!!!*

'Get in!' he roared, punching the air with passion.
The old Dele was definitely back, and so was his
big smile.

At the age of twenty-four, he had already achieved
so much in his career, but he was always hungry

for more. More goals, more assists and more glory. When he made the big move to Tottenham from his boyhood club, MK Dons, he had shown no fear, and with help from Harry and Pochettino, he had proved himself in the Premier League straight away.

From there, Dele's talent and determination had taken him all the way to the 2018 World Cup with England, and the 2019 Champions League Final with Spurs. Although both tournaments had ended in disappointment, Dele wasn't giving up. No way – that wasn't his style. Dele saw every setback as a lesson to be learned, with every step taking him closer to becoming a world-class winner.

DELE ALLI HONOURS

MK Dons
🏆 Football League One runner-up: 2014–15

Tottenham
🏆 UEFA Champions League runner-up: 2018–19

Individual
🏆 Football League Young Player of the Year: 2014–15
🏆 Milton Keynes Dons Players' Player of the Year: 2014–15
🏆 BBC Goal of the Season: 2015–16
🏆 PFA Young Player of the Year: 2015–16, 2016–17

DELE ALLI

20

THE FACTS

NAME: Bamidele Jermaine Alli

DATE OF BIRTH: 11 April 1996

AGE: 24

PLACE OF BIRTH: Milton Keynes

NATIONALITY: England

BEST FRIEND: Harry Hickford

CURRENT CLUB: Tottenham

POSITION: CAM

THE STATS

Height (cm):	188
Club appearances:	307
Club goals:	86
Club trophies:	1
International appearances:	37
International goals:	3
International trophies:	0
Ballon d'Ors:	0

 HERO RATING: 86

GREATEST MOMENTS

 **26 AUGUST 2014,
MK DONS 4–0 MANCHESTER UNITED**

Dele had already made a name for himself in League
One, but this was the night he proved himself against
Premier League opponents. Although he didn't
score or set up any of the goals, Dele outplayed the
whole Manchester United midfield, at the age of
only eighteen. It was a classy cup performance that
really impressed Mauricio Pochettino, the Tottenham
manager.

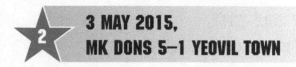

3 MAY 2015,
MK DONS 5–1 YEOVIL TOWN

After signing for Spurs, Dele went straight back to
MK Dons on loan. He was determined to get his
hometown club promoted and this was the day he
did it. Dele didn't score or set up any goals, but
he dominated in midfield. Plus, he had already
contributed sixteen goals and nine assists that season.
This was the perfect way to say goodbye to the Dons.

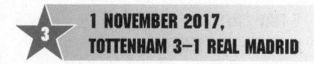

1 NOVEMBER 2017,
TOTTENHAM 3–1 REAL MADRID

Dele already had a reputation as a big game player,
and he confirmed it here against Cristiano Ronaldo's
Real Madrid in the Champions League at Wembley.
He slid in bravely to score the first goal, used his skills
to score the second, and then helped set up the third
for Christian Eriksen. To cap off a perfect performance,
Dele even gave Sergio Ramos the nutmeg treatment!

7 JULY 2018, SWEDEN 0–2 ENGLAND

Up until this point, it had been a frustrating first World Cup for Dele. He had to miss England's last two group games because of injury. Although he returned against Colombia, this was the game when Dele announced he was really back. With England 1–0 up, he made his classic back-post run to head home Jesse Lingard's cross and secure their place in the semi-finals.

8 MAY 2019, AJAX 2–3 TOTTENHAM

On this miraculous night, Tottenham pulled off an incredible Champions League comeback to make it through to the final. At half-time, 2–0 down, it looked all over for Spurs, but Dele didn't give up. He started the fightback by setting up the first goal for Lucas Moura and he finished it by doing the same again. With the last kicks of the game, Dele flicked a clever pass through to Lucas, who fired in the winner and completed a hat-trick.

PLAY LIKE YOUR HEROES

BURST INTO THE BOX LIKE DELE ALLI

STEP 1: Battle bravely for the ball in the middle of the pitch, using all your strength and determination.

STEP 2: Once your team have it back, go go go!

STEP 3: When the ball goes out wide, start making your move towards the back-post area. Take your time, though – you want to catch your opponents by surprise!

STEP 4: As the cross comes in, make your big burst into the box, in between two defenders.

STEP 5: If the ball's coming in low, stretch out your leg and slide in if you have to. *BANG!*

STEP 6: If the ball's coming in high, watch it carefully all the way and time your jump. *BOOM!*

STEP 7: *GOAL!* With a mischievous grin on your face, celebrate in a cool way that the kids will want to copy.

TEST YOUR KNOWLEDGE

QUESTIONS

1. Who was Dele's first football hero?

2. What were the MK Dons called up until 2004?

3. How old was Dele when he moved in permanently with the Hickfords?

4. Who predicted that Dele was 'going to be a superstar'?

5. Dele scored on his senior MK Dons debut – true or false?

6. Name at least three members of the Manchester United team that Dele's MK Dons thrashed 4–0 in 2014.

7. How much did Tottenham pay to sign Dele in 2015?

8. Which manager handed Dele his England debut?

9. Tottenham finished second in the Premier League for two years in a row – 2015–16 and 2016–17. Which teams won those titles?

10. Who set up Dele's goal against Sweden at the 2018 World Cup?

11. Dele set up two goals in Tottenham's 2019 Champions League semi-final against Ajax but which of his teammates scored a hat-trick?

Answers below. . . No cheating!

1. *Steven Gerrard* 2. *Wimbledon* 3. *Thirteen* 4. *MK Dons manager Karl Robinson* 5. *False – but he did score a screamer in his second appearance!* 6. *Any of the following: David de Gea, Johnny Evans, Michael Keane, Nick Powell, Anderson, Shinji Kagawa, Danny Welbeck, Chicharito* 7. *£5 million* 8. *Roy Hodgson* 9. *Leicester City and Chelsea* 10. *Jesse Lingard* 11. *Lucas Moura*

CAN'T GET ENOUGH OF
Ultimate Football Heroes?

Check out heroesfootball.com for quizzes, games, and competitions!

Plus join the Ultimate Football Heroes Fan Club to score exclusive content and be the first to hear about new books and events.
https://heroesfootball.com/subscribe/